No. 878
$8.95

SEWING WITH SCRAPS

BY PHYLLIS GUTH & GEORGENA GOFF

TAB BOOKS
Blue Ridge Summit, Pa. 17214

FIRST EDITION

FIRST PRINTING—APRIL 1977

Copyright © 1977 by TAB BOOKS

Printed in the United States
of America

Library of Congress Cataloging in Publication Data

Guth, Phyllis.
    Sewing with scraps.

    1. Sewing. 2. Textile fabrics. I. Goff,
Georgeanna, joint author. II. Title.
TT715.G82   646.4   77-1782
ISBN 0-8306-7878-6
ISBN 0-8306-6878-0 pbk.

To our mothers, who taught us that thrift
is not necessarily an *old-fashioned* virtue.

Contents

Foreword

If you're as guilty as we are of saying "I'm not going to buy any more fabric until I use up the pieces I already have," then you'll understand why this book was written. We hope it will inspire you to take a second look at the material you have squirreled away and dig out all your leftover scraps and bargain remnants.

Although many of the ideas in this book were developed as a means of saving money by utilizing remnants already on hand, some persons might like to try the suggested methods solely to create original-looking clothes that would be hard to duplicate.

If you are a beginner at sewing or have not as yet acquired the habit of saving your scraps, you might have to purchase small amounts of fabric in different colors and designs to use in the patchwork. Even at that, you should still save money in sewing the garment since the store-bought cost of a similar item would be much higher because of labor and markups.

If you don't have scraps, you might have a friend who would be willing to give you hers. Or you might want to do as Georgena did and buy scraps by the pound if they're available in your area. Of course you don't want to overlook fabric departments where cuts of less than 1 yard often can be picked up quite reasonably.

If you have some but not all of the material on hand to make a garment from scraps, you can still save by using those you have and buying only the amounts of coordinating material necessary to complete it. To determine how much

5

fabric you'll need, lay the pattern pieces that you'll have to buy fabric for on the lengthwise grain of another piece of fabric or sheeting and measure off the amount required. You gain because you only have to purchase material for those pattern pieces rather than for the whole garment. In order to be certain of getting a good match for the fabric you have on hand, carry swatches with you when you go to buy material.

A word about patterns: because of rapidly changing styles, it is unlikely that you'll find patterns exactly like those shown in this book. We hope that this won't discourage you from trying to implement our ideas in your sewing. You will find styles that are similar in some respects. For instance, a skirt with a front panel that would allow for patchwork inserts might be shorter or longer, but the style would remain basically the same. And although you might not find a pattern for a culottes dress, this shouldn't stop you from inserting a contrasting yoke, sleeves, or center front inset in a dress that is made along similar lines.

One chapter in this book deals with items that you can make from remnants which don't involve any sewing at all. We felt, however, that the ideas deserved mention since they do provide a means of putting your scraps to use—turning out novel items that make unusual gifts.

About the use of "I": since this book is a joint effort you might wonder about the use of the singular pronoun in places. These particular instances involved individual endeavors on the part of one, but not both, of us.

This is as good a place as any to qualify something else you'll find in the book. In the chapter on cutting children's clothing costs and again in the one entitled "Partial Patchwork and Other Tricky Techniques" we suggest to the reader that she might try using the fabric on the crosswise rather than the lengthwise grain—in one instance to make a vest and in the other to create an apron effect in a skirt. However, it would be a mistake to assume that you can always lay out your pattern on the crosswise grain and never have disastrous results.

I found this out the hard way when, in order to have the print on the fabric running in a different direction than it would have otherwise, I foolishly placed the pattern for the slacks I was making on the crosswise grain of a polyester knit fabric. Needless to say, the experiment was a total disaster. The first time I sat down, the crotch stretched out of shape. At the same time there was no "give" across the hip area, and this gave the appearance of slacks that were cut a size too small. In the case of the vest and skirt though, the former was sewn from a bonded knit which precluded stretching and the latter called for the use of fabric cut on the crosswise grain only on the skirt front and not in the seat where it might have stretched out of shape. Neither garment was closely fitted to the body.

Some of the material found in this book originally appeared in *Lady's Circle, The Woman, Woman's World, Stitch'n Sew, The Times* supplement to the *Army, Navy, and Air Force Times*, and the *Evening Chronicle* newspaper in Allentown, Pennsylvania. We'd like to take this opportunity to thank the editors of these publications for permission to reprint. We're also grateful to the McCall, Simplicity, Butterick, Kwik-Sew, Let's Make Lingerie, and Sew Lovely Lingerie pattern companies for allowing us to use photos and drawings of clothes and accessories sewn from their patterns.

Thanks also should go to photographers Bob and Mel Thomas whose pictures appear in several of the chapters as well as on the cover and to another friend and photographer, Betty Herring, for the pictures in Chapters 11 and 12.

Beautiful fabrics will always be with us and, inevitably, the leftovers from sewing with them. We hope that this book will enable you to save by using these remnants in other sewing projects. We also hope that you'll be sufficiently inspired to sort through all those scraps you've been saving over the years (your spouse might not know about them and your kids might not be aware of them, but we know!) and to put them to work for you.

Georgena Goff
Phyllis Guth

Introduction:
Get Set to Sew

Home sewing, once you've cleared the hurdle of the initial investment in a good sewing machine, does not call for a lot of expensive items. It goes without saying, of course, that you'll need a sharp pair of scissors, a pattern, thread, fabric, and whatever notions are called for in the pattern. A host of accessories are available to the home sewer, but aside from a few essentials, these are not an absolute necessity.

Like the purchase of any other major appliance, the acquisition of a sewing machine requires some forethought and planning. For instance, before buying one you should decide if you want a machine that offers a stretch as well as a zigzag stitch. Sewing machines featuring the stretch stitch are available in different price ranges. While this particular stitch is nice to use when working with knits, it is by no means essential for sewing with them. And while it would be hard today to find a new sewing machine that cannot be set up to execute a zigzag stitch, you might run across one that does not have this feature if you're planning to buy an older secondhand model, so you might want to inquire about this. The zigzag comes in handy for plain or fancy work, and it is ideal for finishing seams of garments made of loosely woven fabrics that might ravel as well as for mending and reinforcing.

In the store you might be tempted to buy a deluxe model capable of turning out a variety of embroidery stitches. But if you have no plans to use this feature and your pocketbook is slender, it makes more sense to buy a cheaper model without the frills. Also, to be assured of good quality, repair service, and replacement parts if they should be needed, we would recommend buying a machine bearing a well-known name even if it means making do with a no-nonsense model.

You'll also have to decide between a cabinet or a portable model. If space is at a premium in your present apartment or home, you might want to consider buying a portable machine to start with. This can be set up on the kitchen table when you want to use it and stored in a closet the rest of the time. On the other hand, if lack of space is no problem, you might prefer to invest in a cabinet model. Cabinets come in a variety of styles and finishes that blend with modern or traditional furnishings and, although one of these attractive models would fit in a bedroom, living room, or wherever else you care to set it, you'll probably want to put it where the light is best.

All cabinets are not necessarily expensive; it is still possible to purchase an inexpensive hardwood one. Be advised though that the cheaper models do not always have drawer space in them, although sewing chairs with storage room in the seat for thread spools are available. More luxurious cabinets will naturally cost more, but if you consider that the cabinet will be part of the furnishings in your home, the initial cost will not seem great. Incidentally, if you buy a floor model cabinet, you can sometimes buy the more deluxe style for about the same price a smaller-size cabinet would cost brand new.

The notions department is the place to shop for buttons, scissors, zippers, thread, elastic, and sewing accessories such as seam rippers, cutting boards, sleeve boards, tracing wheels, and tailor's hams. Confusion could be the order of the day when you wander unprepared into the notions department, so let's sort things out.

Cutting boards, for instance, can make laying out a pattern considerably easier because of the markings printed on the board, but it is possible to cut out fabric on a tabletop (although I wouldn't recommend doing this on a table with an expensive finish).

A seam ripper is one item I would not be without. It can be bought for under $1 and is used for opening up the tiny stitches that make up a machine-stitched seam. A tailor's ham is used when pressing a curved seam, and a sleeve board is used for ironing just that as well as for ironing other small sections of a garment.

A tracing wheel is used in combination with a special paper to mark the position of darts, tucks, pockets, and so forth, but such markings also can be made with tailor's tacks in a contrasting color of thread. Different types of dress forms are available for those who prefer to work with them. Look them over at your local department store or fabric center to see which type suits you and your budget before buying one.

Many types of scissors are on the market in prices ranging from moderate to fairly expensive. In selecting yours, make certain you choose a pair that open and close smoothly. Keep them sharp by using them only to cut fabric.

For cutting out the fabric, you'll need a dressmaker type of shears, but for cutting threads and buttonholes, smaller scissors are preferable. Pinking shears are nice to own but are not absolutely essential since they are not often used for cutting out the material but rather for finishing seams of fabrics that tend to ravel.

Electric scissors make the difficult task of cutting through wools and corduroys appreciably easier. However, if you don't own a pair, you can manage by laying out the pattern pieces on a single thickness of material when working with heavy fabrics rather than the double thickness that is generally called for. If you do this, though, it is important to remember to turn either the pattern or the fabric to the opposite side when cutting out the pattern pieces the second time. If you don't, you are going to end up with two left dress fronts and, as a result, you might find yourself in the position of not having enough fabric left to cut the extra pieces you need.

Summing up, home sewing can provide the means for keeping the cost of clothing your family at a minimum. And it is possible to do this without investing a lot of money in accessories, although the person who intends to spend a great deal of time sewing might feel justified in purchasing extra equipment because of the added convenience and the time saved. The choice is up to you.

Best Buys in Fabrics

Sewing and saving go hand in hand, but in order to obtain the best fabric buys it's important to know where and when to buy materials and then how to put them to use, right down to the smallest scrap. Remember that large pieces of leftover material never put to use are actually costing you money, whereas if you combine your remnants in original and creative garments, using the step-by-step methods outlined in this book, not only will you be saving dollars but you'll receive compliments on your distinctive outfits as well.

Knowing when to buy fabrics is important because materials, like wearing apparel, are seasonal and as such are removed from the shelves four times a year to be replaced by bolts of fabric suitable for the coming season. Those seasonal yard goods that aren't sold at the time of the changeover are usually reduced in price. What's more, the higher-priced goods often carry the most drastic reductions. And since the fabric is apt to be sale-priced midway through the season it is intended for, usually there is ample time left to sew it up and wear the dress or pantsuit made from the material that same year.

If this is not the case, I simply store the fabric in my cedar chest or other safe place until the following year. You can do this with almost any fabric, and it will not look out-of-date when sewn up a year later, provided you use a pattern for a currently popular style or one that has classic lines which are always in fashion. The only exception to this rule would be fad fabrics, so generally I avoid them.

11

When do you look for good buys in fabrics? During the months between Christmas and Easter you can find fabrics such as woolens, heavy knits, jerseys, felt, velvets, and holiday brocades on sale. Pastel acrylics, lightweight wools, and other spring fabrics are usually reduced in price after Easter, making this a good time to buy your fabric for next year's spring outfit. After the Fourth of July look for cottons, polyesters in summer shades and weights, and sheer fabrics at special prices. Corduroys and dark cottons can often be bought at a reduced price late in fall or at the time the glittery holiday fabrics are put out on the shelves.

Fabrics are not the only items sale-priced at certain times of the year; decorative trims and appliques are also put on sale periodically. For instance, the very expensive sequined and beaded trims used in making gala holiday outfits are sometimes sold at a special price after Christmas, so if you buy coordinated trim and fabric at this time, you can make a glamorous dress or hostess gown far more cheaply than it would otherwise cost.

Zippers, too, can be bought inexpensively. The cheaper zippers are usually sold "loose" without a wrapper and are priced according to length in most stores. By purchasing these lower-priced zippers, I figure that I save 25 to 50 cents on the price of each garment I sew. The quality is excellent, and I've never experienced any problems with them.

Save, too, on polyester thread by stocking up on large-sized spools in basic colors when it's offered at a special price. It seems as if you can never have too much thread on hand if you do a lot of sewing and mending. And if you happen to buy a shade that it turns out you have no use for, you can always use it to make tailor's tacks and for basting purposes.

In your search for reasonably priced materials, don't disregard the better fabric sections of the department stores. The best buys are often found there. At department store rummage sales, for instance, you can sometimes get marvelous buys on short pieces of fabric. And if you're lucky enough to find two, three, or four matching remnants, you might even have enough fabric for a pants and top outfit at a cost of just a few dollars—if you figure on 50 or 75 cents for each piece.

Don't overlook special sales on fabric that stores feature from time to time. Watch for newspaper advertisements of these sales and sign up to receive advance notice of such events at stores which offer this service. Be a comparison shopper, too, and shop around, checking prices at fabric stores, mill outlets, discount houses, and department stores.

You might be surprised at the price difference at various stores handling the same type of fabrics. Also check these stores for remnants which often can be picked up quite reasonably.

In one instance, by comparison shopping I was able to buy slipcover material at a discount house in a nearby town for $1 a yard less than the identical fabric was selling for in a local store. Buying the fabric out of town in this case saved about $15 because of the many yards of material needed, although I wouldn't recommend traveling a great distance when only 1 or 2 yards are required.

Although they're usually cheaper at a discount house, sturdy fabrics suitable for slipcovers or furniture throws are, as a general rule, expensive. But if you buy an all-purpose fabric such as corduroy, which is equally at home on a drapery rod or couch or made up into clothing, you can save money. What's more, since corduroy is washable you won't have any dry-cleaning bills with this type of fabric. For best results, preshrink before using.

The price of fine quality drapery fabrics could be enough to make you seek out the store-bought variety. One solution to this is to shop for such fabrics when they're on sale or, as in the case of the slipcover fabric, to buy at a discount store offering lower prices. Another solution is to use dress fabrics to curtain windows. It is doubtful if you could do this in every room of the house, but it is possible to curtain the kitchen, bathroom, and bedroom windows with fabric intended for making garments. At a fabric sale I once bought a sheer, dotted dress fabric which made up into crisp, attractive curtains at a fraction of the price it would have cost me to make them otherwise. Here's a good rule to keep in mind: "Don't be afraid to use fabrics in new ways."

If you have a mill outlet store in your town that sells fabrics, be sure to check its prices on polyester knits, particularly when there is a sale in progress. An outlet store, conveniently located near my home, often sells polyesters for anywhere from $1 to $3 a yard. These are the same bolts of fabric that would ordinarily sell elsewhere for $3 to $6 a yard, so although I buy them cheaply, I know that I am getting a true bargain.

A word of warning though: before you buy sale material, check it over for flaws, particularly if it is a precut piece. Obviously, a large flaw running the length of the goods is no bargain, while a slightly soiled piece is, provided the stain is not of a permanent nature. And by careful placement of your pattern, you can usually cut around a small hole or flaw if you allow yourself a little extra fabric for leeway at the time of purchase.

When buying remnants, beware of off-grain prints. These will come to light if you grasp the selvadges in your hands and hold the piece of material at arm's length, letting a yard or so dangle. Examine the material across from left to right, and if the print or weave runs downhill rather than straight across, you'll know that's probably the reason that particular piece is on the remnant pile. Should you by chance buy such a piece of fabric, you'll find that if you cut it with the grain the print will run on a slant, while if you cut the dress following the lines of the print you won't be cutting on the grainline as the pattern directions call for. Therefore, avoid such fabrics even at bargain prices.

Sheets are another potential source of reasonably priced material for use in sewing. While the delicate floral prints on a white background might be more suitable for making dusters or robes, there are other prints that could be used to sew anything from shower curtains to women's dresses and children's clothing. The ever-popular checks, for instance, would look equally at home in a kitchen, bathroom, or bedroom or could be made up into wearing apparel.

If you select a flat sheet with a contrasting hem, you might even be able to work the hem into whatever it is you're making. And for truly great buys, watch for price reductions on sheets, particularly when they're offered at rummage sales. Often at such sales there aren't too many of one kind, and a complete matched set of sheets is not always available. But unless you're curtaining a whole room and need several of a kind, this could work to your advantage in being able to buy yards of quality fabric at a low price.

You also can save money on patterns by buying discontinued ones, if they're available, at mill outlet stores. Or if your local shops run sales on current patterns, it would probably pay you to do your pattern buying for the season then at low sale prices. Because the styles of garments such as Halloween costumes, maternity dresses, separates, pajamas, robes, and children's overalls do not change as frequently or as drastically as others, it makes good sense to buy discontinued patterns for them.

Which comes first, the pattern or the fabric? I've found that it can be either one. You may have had the experience of coming upon a beautiful length of fabric which you couldn't resist, although you may have had no immediate plans to use it. Other times it might be a particular style of pattern that attracts you. Whichever way you do it, what counts in the end is the way you mate your fabric and pattern.

14

After making your fabric purchase, remember that in order to get the most for your dollar it's important that you use as much of the material as possible. So hang onto any sizable pieces of fabric leftover from your sewing projects. By sizable I mean pieces large enough to provide a patch such as the kind found on a crazy quilt. Fabric leftovers can form the foundation for a new kind of sewing—sewing from scraps. You might even be able to obtain larger size leftover pieces by varying the pattern layout slightly from the one given in the instruction sheet. However, don't disregard such important items as nap and grainlines in your eagerness to get more out of your fabric.

To sum it up briefly, if you shop for fabric and other sewing needs with an eye toward economy, you'll find that you can come up with genuine bargains. And if you hold onto your sewing scraps as well and put them to use in the ways recommended in this book, you'll realize still greater savings and at the same time come up with a wardrobe that can't be surpassed in originality. Start now to see what good buys in fabrics and accessories you can seek out and sew.

Two Fabrics Are Better Than One

What do I use the fabrics for? That's the big question. Let's suppose you got carried away at a fabric sale and bought several pieces of material but haven't the faintest idea how you're going to use them. Before admitting defeat and donating them to the rescue mission, try looking at the remnants in a new light.

Let's say, for instance, you bought a cotton print that you originally thought would make up into a lovely blouse but you now realize that you don't have anything to wear with it. Or it might be that you're not so certain now that it would make a nice blouse anyway. However, you do have some scraps that would blend with that particular piece, but not quite enough of one kind to make an entire garment. If this is the case, try sewing a model's coat for around-the-house wear. Use the print fabric that was previously intended for a blouse to make the main sections of the coat (actually a duster). Then take your coordinating scraps and use them for the cap sleeves, patch pockets, and yoke.

Or perhaps you purchased a piece of fabric for a skirt and again have nothing to wear with it. However, you do have a length of white fabric on hand, so why not combine the two in a dress? Use the white for the bodice and the heavier fabric for the skirt. You might even bring into play a third fabric, depending on the style of the dress. I once snapped up a piece of olive green fabric at a bargain price, intending to sew a skirt from it, only to change my mind later. As it turned out, I ended up combining the green fabric with a linen-like white one from my remnant drawer. For contrast, I used strips of a quilted orange, tan, and green print. The result is pictured in Fig. 2-1. You probably won't find a pattern exactly like this, but don't let that stop you from making similar combinations using another pattern.

When I ended up with a piece of polyester fabric in a red-orange plaid after sewing a pair of slacks, I hated to see the lovely fabric go to waste, yet I didn't have enough for a complete garment. By laying out a pattern on the leftover fabric I found, however, that I did have enough material to sew the front sections of a button-front skirt. So I shopped for a solid color polyester in a matching shade to make the skirt back and the waistband. I also happened to have on hand a small amount of furry fabric in the same ecru shade that formed a background for the plaid, and I used this to sew the pockets. The end result was the attractive, sporty-looking skirt shown in Fig. 2-2.

You can often pick up new ideas for using up your remnants by looking around in the ready-to-wear sections of

Fig. 2-1. Two purchased remnants plus some quilted fabric leftover from another sewing project went into making this dress. The yoke is white linen as are the sleeves. The remainder of the dress is sewn from an olive green acrylic with the quilted bands separating the dress sections. (Courtesy of the McCall Pattern Company.)

Fig. 2-2. A red-orange plaid and matching solid color fabric team up in this button-front shirt. The skirt front features patch pockets cut from fake fur.

department stores. For instance, long-sleeved blouses are sometimes made from two fabrics with the sleeves and collars cut from one print and the bodices from the coordinating one. You would have to proceed cautiously, however, and not just throw any two fabrics together simply to use them up. You may already have one print on hand but not enough of it to complete the entire garment, and will therefore have to purchase the needed amount of coordinating material. Even with the purchase of the extra material included, the garment will still only cost you half as much to make because of the bonus remnant you already had.

Another trick designers employ involves the use of two like fabrics but with the colors reversed such as a blue and white floral design used with the same print in white and blue. You could combine two such fabrics effectively in making a long skirt with a flounce by sewing the skirt in one print and the flounce in the opposite-colored one.

In order to combine fabrics successfully it is important that all the materials used in one garment are compatible in dry-cleaning or laundering qualities. Therefore, know what it is that you're buying, because today acrylics can masquerade as wool. Also, it's sometimes difficult to tell just by looking at it whether the fabric is washable or not. When you purchase material right off the bolt you should receive a sticker with laundering or dry-cleaning instructions on it. But when you pick up a remnant, this kind of information isn't always available. If I'm not certain of the wool content, if any, of a fabric, I take the precaution either of putting the garment sewn from it into a coin-operated dry-cleaning machine or else I launder it by hand in cold water, using a soap designed for wool fabrics. It is possible to use wool with acrylics (I did so in making a patchwork purse for winter use), but I would never toss an item made from such a combination into the washing machine because of the wool content in it.

It's often said that prevention is the best medicine, and to prevent shrinkage problems from arising I run washable fabrics through the rinse cycle on my washing machine before I ever cut into them. In doing so, I shrink the material (if it's going to shrink) before the fabric is sewn up. And if you plan to dry the garment you're making from the fabric in the clothes dryer, you might as well toss the material into the dryer at this time, too. This method should virtually eliminate the chance of any further reduction in the size of the fabric. By treating your washable fabrics at the outset, you won't have to worry when you combine various fabrics in one garment, either in patchwork fashion or otherwise, that each one will shrink individually and possibly cause puckers.

When buying fabric to sew a suit or pantsuit, it might pay you to purchase the extra yardage necessary to sew the additional piece needed to make the suit three-piece. That way the top you buy or make to go with the skirt can be worn with the pants and, of course, the jacket also can team up with both the skirt and pants. Here again you can put fabric combinations into play either by using what you have on hand and buying coordinating fabric to match or by purchasing two harmonizing fabrics.

A store which carries a full selection of a line of fabrics will sometimes display the coordinating prints and solids side by side, thus enabling you to tell at a glance what goes together. I once sewed a jacket from a floral miniprint and slacks from the coordinating design. When worn with a white turtleneck sweater, the combination was very effective. I then went a step further and used remnants from both along with a yard of a solid color fabric bought to match and combined them in a culotte dress. The print jacket also could be worn over the dress, proving that the possibilities are almost endless when you build your wardrobe or part of it around coordinates.

Still another combination of fabrics is possible in making a pantsuit, as witnessed by Fig. 2-3. I hit upon this idea involving

Fig. 2-3. Two fabrics went into this pantsuit. The sleeves, collar, and front of the pant top were cut from a pink cotton. A purple print provided the fabric for the back of the pant top, pockets, and slacks. The figure at the left is a back view of the top. (Courtesy of the McCall Pattern Company.)

the use of dual fabrics after buying fabric for the pants, only to discover that I had a pink remnant on hand that would be an ideal match to the predominately purple print of the pants fabric, but with a hint of pink in it. The hitch was that I didn't have enough of the pink fabric for the entire top, and this outfit was the result of my making do with what was on hand. The sleeves, collar, and front sections of the pantsuit top were cut from the solid pink fabric with the back of the pantsuit top and the pants made from the print.

Now and then you might have the experience of finding a particular color material that appeals to you but, alas, you cannot wear it because of your coloring. In my case I was drawn to an olive green print but knew instinctively that with my pale complexion it was not my best color. The print featured tiny flowers in a tomato red and beige, so I went ahead and bought the fabric anyway but also purchased beige fabric in the same type of material. I then used the green print to make a dress, and cut the collar sections from the beige fabric. With the beige collar framing my face, I was able to wear that shade of green successfully. The dress is pictured at the left in Fig. 2-4.

You can also brighten up a plain navy or black dress by trimming it with white. The result can be very striking. Carry this idea one step further and use white thread to do whatever topstitching is called for on the black or navy fabric. Ecru is another shade that can be used to sew contrasting color collars, cuffs, yokes, and the like.

When selecting material for a contrast collar, don't make the mistake of choosing a limp fabric to use with a firmly woven one. Nothing could look worse. It makes far better sense to buy the necessary small amount of fabric for the collar than to ruin the appearance of the garment you're making by using an unsuitable remnant. Also be sure to take

Fig. 2-4. Two different versions of the same pattern. The dress at the left is shown made up with short sleeves and a constrasting collar, while the bodice at the right is sewn from one fabric and the skirt from another. (Both dresses shown through the courtesy of the Butterick Pattern Service.)

21

note of the various shades of white that are available and then to buy the proper one for the color you're using.

Choosing the right shade can make a big difference in the end. If you're using a print fabric to make the outfit, let the colors in it serve as a guide as to what shade to use for contrast. For instance, if ecru appears in the print, then select ecru for the collar rather than a true white. Generally speaking, different shades of brown and green blend well with beige, while navy, black, and red are often used in combination with white.

Because of its waistline seam and shirtdress styling, the pattern used in sewing the print dress also lends itself to the use of different fabrics in making the bodice and skirt. The dress shown at the right in Fig. 2-4 features a red and white flocked gingham check bodice and a pastel blue skirt with red buttons parading down the dress front. You could also use the same type of pattern in a long-sleeved version to make a dress with a white bodice and a skirt cut from a dark print. For an added touch, cut the collar and cuffs too from the print fabric.

Bold and vivid prints can be beautiful and a delight to work with. But in order to achieve a kind of balance where one such print stands out from the others, I use the flashy fabric to cut the smaller sections of the garment or to highlight inconspicuous places where that print won't steal the show from the other less striking designs. One example of this is the duster shown in Fig. 2-5. It is made from a black-and-white fabric; a yellow, white, and black print; and a white fabric featuring flowers that are outlined in black. Notice that the bolder, black design was used in making the cap sleeves and pockets while the more prominent sections of the garment were sewn from the other fabrics.

In putting these three fabrics together, color was not the only factor involved. The materials met another requirement in that all three were permanent press cottons of about the same weight. Incidentally, if you still have fabric on hand that isn't permanent press, I'd avoid using it in combination with fabrics that are. Otherwise, you'll end up with a garment which will require partial pressing.

The smock shown in Fig. 2-6, a short version of the duster, features no less than four recycled or leftover fabrics and was originally made as part of an artist costume for a Halloween party. A cornflower blue print, cut from an old "granny gown," provided the material for the front yoke sections. A print in a matching color was used to make the pockets, while the yoke back was cut from a pastel blue fabric. Pale blue gingham in a fine check was used for the remainder of the

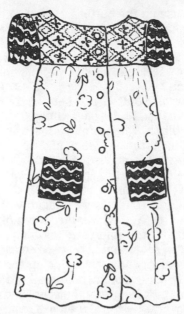

Fig. 2-5. This duster or "model's coat" was sewn from a smock pattern with extra length added. The color scheme is yellow, black, and white. (© 1975 Simplicity Pattern Company.)

garment. The costume cost me next to nothing to make, and I had the added bonus of being able to wear the smock afterward to protect my clothes while cooking or working on messy crafts or refinishing projects.

"Button, button, who's got the button?" You probably do, and lots of them if you're like us and salvage them from discarded clothing. A word of caution though: when gathering up your fabric remnants to use in a garment you might feel

Fig. 2-6. This short smock was made from four different blue fabrics that harmonize with one another. (© 1975 Simplicity Pattern Company.)

that you want to use up the buttons in your collection, too. This could be a mistake because an otherwise lovely outfit can be spoiled by the use of the wrong type of buttons. Therefore, we feel that we are justified in spending the extra dollar or so if necessary to buy the right kind of buttons for whatever it is that we are sewing.

Just as the wrong button can detract from a garment, so the proper one can turn it into something unique. For instance, if you're using a black, white, and yellow print or combination of fabrics, look for buttons in black and white or in yellow and white. And when you're baffled, don't take the easy route by selecting an all white button. Pick up one of the colors in the print, and match the buttons to it. You can also use a trick that is sometimes used in ready-to-wear clothes. If you're sewing an outfit in navy blue and white, buy cards of buttons in both navy and white but of the same size and shape. Then alternate the colors when you sew them in place. You can also transform a store-bought coat or suit by replacing the buttons. I once purchased a pale blue poplin coat that was trimmed with unattractive, cheap-looking gold buttons. With the addition of pastel blue and white buttons, the coat took on a whole new look and at a minimal cost.

Most of the same rules pertaining to combining fabrics in one garment also apply to patchwork. The success of your patchwork design, however, is also dependent upon the designs in the patches used as well as the placement of them. For instance, a large splashy design would probably look out of place alongside small-scale calico prints. Fabric scraps having large scale designs on them can be successfully used in patchwork, too, but they can be appreciated more readily in a large size patch.

When it comes to the type of fabrics used in patchwork, I personally prefer to work with cotton because it doesn't twist out of shape or curl at the edges. One exception to this was the patchwork purse made from wool and acrylic fabrics shown in Chapter 7. Also, I find that the availability of a wide variety of both figured and plain cottons and cotton blends makes the job of finding coordinating fabrics that much easier.

There's no need to stick to safe and prosaic combinations such as yellow and green or red and blue when putting your patchwork together. Be daring and different. Use varying shades of blue, and throw in a little green and white for contrast. Try a salmon shade with white and black prints. For fall, make a patchwork in gold, green, and rust or brown colors. Sew up a pastel patchwork for summertime, and welcome the spring with a red, white, and blue trio of checks, plaids, and solids. The use of intense or dark colors with white or light shades can lead to disastrous results when the garment made from such a combination is laundered, so take the precaution of testing the dark fabrics first to see if they're colorfast.

Patchwork can be used not only to make an entire garment, but also to trim clothing sewn from conventional fabrics. Moreover, patchwork trim and a combination of fabrics can be used in the same dress or jacket or whatever the case may be, as the jacket shown in Figure 2-7 demonstrates. Because of the variety of materials used in the jacket, it lends itself to a number of possible combinations. For instance, the jacket could be worn with a skirt, pants, or dress made from anyone of the fabrics used in the jacket. The red, white, and blue colors in the patchwork, sleeves, and pockets are an effective contrast to the white pique of the jacket.

To make the patchwork band and undercollar in this case, I didn't find it necessary to sew the patches to a backing

Fig. 2-7. The button front band of this white pique jacket was done in patchwork and remnants used to sew the sleeves and pockets. The top collar section is white while the undersection of collar, which is an extension of band, is patched. You could reverse this to have a patchwork collar and plain band if you desire. (Courtesy of Butterick Pattern Service.)

25

because the piece needed was so small. (See Chapter 6, "Patching Up Your Gift List," for instructions on sewing the patches to a backing.) Instead I seamed the patches together to make a strip shaped like the band, adding ⅝ in. for the seam allowance at the top where the band joins with the undercollar. Then I cut the undercollar sections separately rather than all in one with the front band as the pattern called for, but making an allowance for the seam needed to connect the two pieces. Although the undercollar was cut from a larger piece of the same fabric used in the patchwork, I chose not to patch it because the results wouldn't be seen when the garment was sewn together. The top collar sections and band facings are made from white pique.

As you can see from this chapter, two fabrics can be better than one, and three would never be considered a crowd, provided you have the right combination of materials. So scavenge in your scrap drawer, rummage through your remnants, save your scraps, and see what unique outfits you can come up with.

Elegant "Block" Skirts 3

The pretty floor-length skirt pictured in Fig. 3-1 was made from leftover pieces of sewing fabrics. If you use lightweight materials such as single knits or cottons, you might want to cut a backing for your "blocks." I did. The sheeting I used not only made the skirts hang better but eliminated the need for a slip.

All the adult block skirts shown in this chapter will fit sizes 10 to 14. If you are shorter than 5 ft 3 in., shorten all your pattern pieces by 1 in.

THE MIDLENGTH SKIRT

The material used for the midlength skirt shown in Fig. 3-2, left, was purchased at a fabric sale. At 77 cents a yard I couldn't resist two, 45 in. wide fabrics that looked as if they would combine beautifully. After I had found a third piece of material which would coordinate well with the other two (at $1.19 a yard), I bought 1 yard of each of the three fabrics. For this skirt I also bought 9 yards of brown seam lace to outline the blocks of this predominately beige skirt. (I chose seam lace for this skirt rather than the bias tape I used on the gingham skirt because the muted colors seemed to call for a more delicate touch.)

I shall give directions for making the midlength skirt. The floor-length skirts will be made the same way. The first thing to do is to make your pattern pieces out of paper according to the measurements given in Fig. 3-3. Notice in the sketches that there are two panels of narrow blocks down the front and back

27

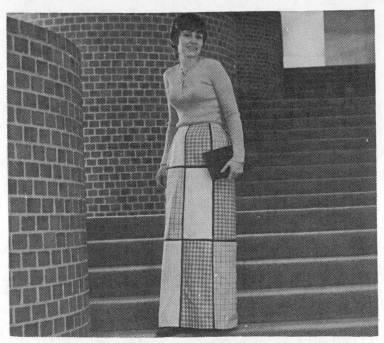
Fig. 3-1. A classic block skirt.

Fig. 3-2. A midlength skirt at left contrasts with a child's floor-length skirt.

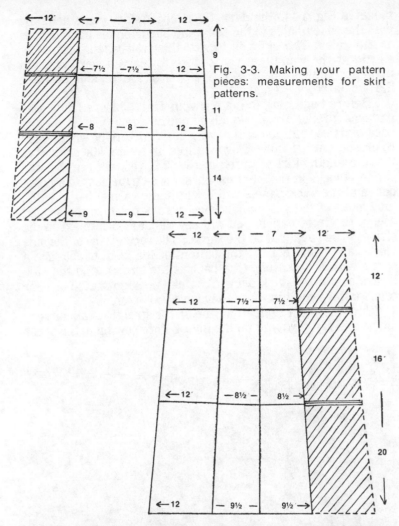

Fig. 3-3. Making your pattern pieces: measurements for skirt patterns.

with each of the four panels made of blocks exactly alike. So you will need to cut only three patterns (one each for the top, middle, and bottom) to make the 12 blocks you will need. Notice that the side panels are of wider blocks than the middle (front and back) panels.

You will need three more patterns, this time for six blocks. You will notice that the tops of all blocks are narrower than the bottoms. When increasing the widths from, say 7 in. at the top to 7½ in. at the bottom, be sure to increase ¼ in. on either side of the block (not ½ in. on one side).

Note: Though I refer to the narrow, "middle" panels, front and back, and the wide "side" panels, you will notice that the model in Fig. 3-4 in the dark, floor-length skirt wears her skirt with the wide panels in the front and back and the narrow ones at the sides. The skirt is turned this way when, instead of elastic at the waistline, you choose to make a waistband. In that case you will insert a 7 in. zipper at the left side between the two narrow top blocks.

Before beginning to cut out your fabric blocks from your patterns, draw a rough sketch on paper of both your front and back skirt so that you will have a clear picture of where each color and pattern goes. For example, in the middle section of the midlength skirt pictured in Fig. 3-2, you will see that the two top blocks in the front panels show a stripe next to a polka dot (and the back panels will be the same). On either side the top blocks of the side panels show a dark print. In the second row of the front panels you will see the dark print next to the stripe. (The back will be the same.) The second row of the side blocks are polka dot. At the bottom of the front panels are a stripe with a polka dot (the back is the same), and the side blocks are of the dark print. To make a rough sketch of your color-pattern combinations may save you error.

Cut your blocks one at a time on the straight grain of your fabric and lay them out on the floor before sewing in the order

Fig. 3-4. Here the model wears her skirt with the wide panels front and back and the narrow panels at the sides.

in which they will be sewn together according to your sketch. For a complete front of your skirt you will need two blocks cut from each pattern. For the back you will need two from each pattern. For the *two* sides you will need two from each side pattern.

When your blocks are all cut out and laid on the floor, front, back, and sides, if you do *not* plan to outline them with trim you can now sew them together in panels: front, sides, and back. Then join the panels with lengthwise seams. If you plan to outline your blocks with lace or tape trim you must apply the trim *before* you sew the blocks together, as in the following instructions.

Cut a piece of lace or tape the length of the bottom of your top front block and sew it, wrong side of lace against right side of block and back from the raw edge about ⅜ in. (If you use bias tape, open out one turned underedge of your single-fold tape and press it flat before sewing that edge to the bottom of the block.)

Topstitch the opposite edge of the trim to the block with matching thread. After the trim is sewn to the bottom of the block, sew this top front block to the middle front block. To be sure that you will be catching in the trim as you make this seam, turn your blocks over so that you can see the first stitching you did and follow that line.

Now sew the trim to the bottom of the middle block ⅜ in. back from that bottom edge. Topstitch the trim at its opposite edge. Join the middle block to the bottom block, keeping the stitching you just did on top as a guide to the joining of the blocks (in order to catch in the edge of the trim you just applied). You have now made one complete front panel. Continue making the other five panels in the same way.

Press the panels so that all seams are pressed toward the bottom of the skirt. Now cut the trim for the full length of all panels, and sew it to the *right*-hand edges of all the panels and ⅜ in. back from those raw edges. Sew the panels together one after the other, fronts, side, backs, side and, then, join the final seam to complete the skirt. When sewing down the length of the panels, be especially careful to watch the crosswise lace or bias tape so that it comes together exactly at all corners, making a neat crosswise trim. Pinning will help.

When the skirt has been sewn together, turn to the wrong side and press all lengthwise seams away from the trim.

Turn under ¼ in. at the top edge of the skirt. Press down and turn it over again to make a 1¼ in. casing, leaving an opening to insert ¾ in. elastic cut 1 in. longer than the waist of the person who will wear the skirt. Sew the elastic together, and close the opening with machine stitching or hand sewing.

Turn under ¼ in. at the bottom of the skirt: press, and turn up a hem to the desired length. Note: If you want to line your skirt, cut duplicate blocks of cotton muslin (or even firm old sheeting) and back each block before sewing. If you use new muslin, shrink before using.

LITTLE GIRL'S DIRNDL

It pays to save small scraps from quilts or other sewing projects when you can utilize them to make a worthwhile and pretty garment. This little skirt is made with a simple quilt block design or, more explicitly, two quilt block designs.

Nine small blocks cut from a cardboard pattern 3½ in. on a side are sewn together to make the "nine block." There is one predominating color (plain pink in the little skirt pictured) that is used in every nine block to make the pattern. The shaded areas in the sketches show where the pink blocks are used. Half the nine blocks will have four pink blocks; the other half will have five pink blocks (see Fig. 3-5). For the entire skirt you will need enough of the predominating color to make 108 blocks. You can cut down a bit on this number (as I did) by using a print or check of your predominating (plain) color for the center block of all those nine blocks that normally require five of the predominating color (see the sketch with double-shaded center block).

I used both. In some blocks I used a pink print for the center block (of those nine blocks with the four pink corners); in the rest I used a pink and white check. That way I needed only 96 plain pink small blocks. For the complete skirt you will need 24 nine-blocks in all, 12 for the front and 12 for the back. This size will fit a little girl from six to nine years old (though you can easily make it larger by extending the length).

In quilts this nine block design is often separated, one block from the other, by strips of plain material. This clearly shows the design, but in Fig. 3-6 I have sewn one nine block to the other, making it an all-over pattern. A nine block of four small pink blocks is sewn next to a nine block with five small pink blocks.

Fig. 3-5. By using a print or check of your predominating color for the center block of all those nine blocks that normally require five of the predominant (plain) color, you can cut down a bit on the number needed.

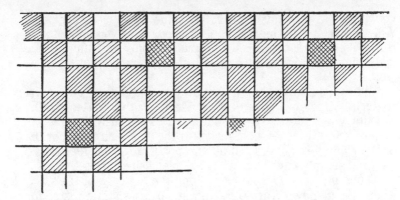

Fig. 3-6. I have sewn one nine block to the other, making it an all-over pattern.

Besides my predominating color of pink, which was a plain color (with the exception of the middle block in half the nine blocks), I had a variety of other colors: prints and checks in yellow, red, orange, fuchsia, green, and blue. This necessitated a careful eye so as not to overuse one colored print or check to the exclusion of some others.

When you begin sewing your small blocks together, carefully restitch at the beginning and end of your blocks. You will sew three small blocks together in a crosswise strip, three more, and three more (with your predominating color in the right places). When you begin to sew these strips of small blocks together to make your nine block, watch carefully so that your corners come together neatly. You can take care of this quite easily by having your seams all the same width. Press all seams open but, to save electricity, make several nine blocks before getting out the iron.

Making several nine blocks is a good idea for another reason. If you have about six nine blocks to lay out on your bed, you will have a choice to begin making the front panel of your skirt. Switch the nine blocks about to find the most attractive combination before sewing together those four nine blocks that will make your middle, front, lengthwise panel.

After your front panel is made, make a few more nine blocks and try them next to the front panel to find the most attractive combinations for your other two front panels. Sew them together. Press the seams open.

To design the back of the skirt you will *not* make a center panel as you did for the front but you will go on from the right-hand side panel of the front. This is so that you can be sure that all your colors are coordinating well. If you find, for example, that you have two many reds and not enough blues, you may have to custom design some of your nine blocks. When you come to the last panel in your skirt you will have to remember to coordinate that panel not only with the middle back panel of your skirt but with the left-hand front panel as well.

What you have been doing is making your own skirt material. However, there is no waste to this material; the amount you make is the amount you use. You will make six panels of four blocks each, three for the front and three for the back. When you have sewn all the panels together and closed the final seam you will be ready to finish your skirt.

Turn under a narrow hem along the top edge of the skirt. About 1½ in. down from that edge make a waistline casing for a drawstring tie by stitching both edges of ⅞ in. bias tape around the skirt. Find the exact middle of the skirt front and make two slits about ½ in. apart over the casing. These openings are for the drawstring tie. Finish the raw edges of the slits with a buttonhole stitch. For the drawstring, buy 2 yards of cording.

Try the skirt on your little girl, and turn up a hem.

Note: If this type of skirt tends to slip down, instead of the drawstring tie, try the following.

Buy some of the wide elastic made especially for skirt bands. Cut it the size of your little girl's waist and attach it to the top of the skirt. Because the elastic will not stretch enough to go around this much material, gather the top of the skirt a bit before sewing on the waistband elastic.

Selecting and Altering for Patchwork

The use of both patchwork and fabric combinations in the things you sew requires some forethought and planning for selecting not only the fabric but also the pattern. To make a garment entirely from patchwork, for instance, you'll want to look for a pattern with few details because of the bulkiness of the patchwork and also to show it off to best advantage. For overall patchwork garments, you'll want to avoid features like princess seaming, gored and pleated skirts, tucks, and ruffles. Instead choose a pattern with relatively simple lines and few seams and darts when planning to make a patchwork skirt, slacks, vest, and so on.

To get ideas for the kind of pattern to use for making a garment from a combination of fabrics, study the pattern catalogs and note the types of patterns made up in contrasting fabrics. If a pattern isn't illustrated in two or more fabrics, don't let that stop you from using a combination of remnants in sewing it if you think the outfit would look attractive that way. In the pattern books you'll find contrasting materials used for yokes, sleeves and collar, collars and cuffs, skirt flounces, front insets, cardigan bands, bodices, and the midriff section of a dress. (These ideas might not all appear in one catalog, however.) You can also use contrasting materials for insets in pant legs, the center front of a dress, button front bands, and the front panel of a skirt.

The pattern for the dress shown in Fig. 4-1 was ideal for contrasting fabrics because of the dropped waistline seam. To make the dress a navy polyester remnant bought quite

Fig. 4-1. Two different fabrics were combined in this dress. The skirt fabric was cut into flower shapes and fused to the bodice with Stitch Witchery. (Courtesy of Butterick Pattern Service.)

inexpensively at a factory outlet was teamed with a red, white, and navy blue plaid acrylic. The acrylic fabric also was used to sew a spring coat to wear over the dress. In order to break up the monotony of the solid navy bodice, I topstitched it in red and added flowers cut from the skirt fabric.

No appliquing is necessary if you use a product such as Stitch Witchery to fuse the two fabrics together. After pressing the flowers in place, I embroidered stems and leaves for each one. When worn together the outfit made an attractive ensemble, yet each also could be worn separately. The acrylic material yielded a bonus, too, in the form of a skirt that I was able to sew from the leftovers.

Pictured in Fig. 4-2 is a dress that could be sewn up in one color or using contrasting fabrics. When made up as shown, however, with contrasting sleeves and collar, the dress resembles a jumper with a blouse under it. The dress can be topstitched in the same shade as the contrasting fabric used in the sleeves and collar.

A skirt pattern such as the one in Fig. 4-3 with a front panel and side pleats can be made from three different pieces of fabric, provided they harmonize. The summery skirt was sewn

Fig. 4-2. This style of dress lends itself to the use of fabric combinations. (© Simplicity Pattern Company.)

entirely from cottons and included a navy blue which was used for the back sections, a medium blue for the side fronts, and a strawberry print on a navy background for the front panel. If you're using remnants, as I did, to make a similar skirt, the size of your fabric pieces could determine whether you'll use them for the front or back sections although you'll naturally want to save the prettiest and most outstanding for the front panel.

Because the navy fabric was lighter in weight than the other two materials used, I realized that I would need a lining in the sections cut from this fabric (the back) in order to compensate. So I dug in my scrap bag and came up with a

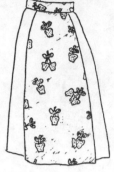

Fig. 4-3. This skirt was sewn from three fabric remnants. The back section is navy and the side sections are a medium blue while the front pleated panel is sewn in a navy print with strawberries scattered on it. (© 1975 Simplicity Pattern Company.)

colorful red, white, and blue cotton print that provided just the amount of fabric necessary to line the back. If your fabric is short of what's needed for the lining, you can make a partial lining instead that extends to a point slightly below the seat of the skirt.

ALTERATIONS

It's fairly simple to make a minor alteration to allow for a contrasting yoke, center front inset, or pant leg insets. To make the proper adjustments on the pattern you'll have to cut the pattern pieces apart that are affected by the changes. However, the pieces can always be taped back together to be used again as originally intended.

The pattern for the culotte dress shown at the left in Fig. 4-4 did not include a contrasting yoke, but it was not a hard change to make. To make this alteration, first decide where the yoke should end and draw a straight line across the bodice front at this point. Then cut the pattern piece apart on the line. When you place these pattern pieces on the fabric though, as in the right illustration of Fig. 4-4, you must remember to add a ⅜ in. seam allowance along the line where you originally cut, both on the yoke and the bodice section. If you place a row of pins on the fabric to mark your new cutting line, you won't be as apt to forget the seam allowances. Seam yoke and bodice, together, press the seam open; then follow pattern instructions to complete the garment. The contrasting yoke permits you to use up your remnants while giving you yet another variation of the pattern. When using a contrasting fabric, though, it's a good idea to cut more than one section of the garment from the contrasting fabric if at all possible. That way the contrasting fabric won't look as if it was tacked on as a last-minute addition.

In this culotte dress the front pant leg sections were cut from the same print used to make the yoke while the back pant legs were sewn in a contrasting print from the same line of fabric. The back and front bodice sections were cut from a matching solid color, while the patchwork panels featured in both the front and back were made entirely from the leftovers of the three fabrics used in the dress.

Shown at the right in Fig. 4-5 is a culotte dress with sleeves sewn from the same pattern. This time, though, the alteration made on the pattern involved the insertion of a contrasting inset that runs down the center front of the bodice. Directions given here are for a dress without a center front seam or front opening of any kind. In order to permit the insertion of the contrasting fabric, the bodice will not be cut on the fold of the material as directed in the pattern and will, with the inset,

TO MAKE CON-
TRASTING YOKE,
CUT PATTERN
APART HERE.

ADD ⅝" TO
EACH CUT EDGE.

Fig. 4-4. The illustration at the left shows how to cut pattern apart. The figure at the right shows culotte dress which was sewn from three coordinating Kettlecloth fabrics, two of them leftover from other projects. The yoke is done in a print, while the bodice is a solid color. The back pant leg sections feature the third print with the culottes sporting patchwork panels sewn from all three fabrics. (© 1975 Simplicity Pattern Company.)

39

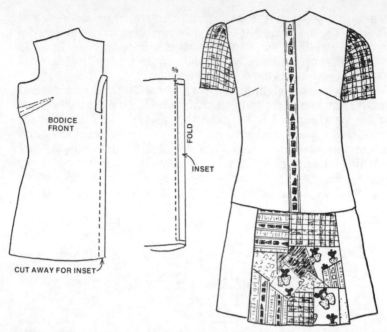

Fig. 4-5. The illustration at the left shows how to cut the bodice pattern piece apart to allow for the center front inset. Place the inset pattern piece along the fold of the fabric as in the center figure. The culotte dress at the right features contrasting sleeves, patchwork panels, and a center front inset. (© 1975 Simplicity Pattern Company.)

have two seams an equal distance apart from the center front of the dress. Here's how to make this change.

First decide how wide you want the finished inset to be and divide this figure in half. Do not include the seam allowance. Next measure from the center front of the bodice pattern, starting at the neckline, and mark off at intervals the amount you arrived at after dividing. Draw a straight line connecting these markings. Cut the pattern apart on this line to make the inset pattern as shown at the left in Fig. 4-5. Pin the inset pattern section on the contrasting fabric, placing the center front on fold as seen in the center illustration of Fig. 4-5. Before cutting it out, measure off and place pins ⅝ in. away from the long edge of the inset where it was cut from the bodice section. Use pins as your guide when cutting out the long side of the inset.

When you pin the bodice section to the fabric, do *not* place it along the fold. And remember to add ⅝ in. to the side where the inset section was cut away so that you'll have the necessary seam allowance. Sew the inset between the bodice fronts; then follow the pattern instructions to finish the dress.

As with the first culotte dress, a third fabric—a red and white flocked gingham check in this case—was brought into play and used for the sleeves. The dress bodice is made from white pique as are the pant leg fronts. The front inset is cut from a red, white, and blue seersucker, while the pant leg backs are sewn in the same fabric but in a solid blue color. The dress sports red, white, and blue patchwork panels in the front and back and can be teamed with the pique jacket shown in Chapter 2.

This last alteration involves cutting apart both front and back pant leg sections at the bottom, to permit a contrasting inset that will match the fabric of the blouse you'll be wearing with the pants (see Fig. 4-6). You could also make the inset from patchwork. The inset is made as follows.

First determine approximately where the hemline of the pants will be by holding the pattern piece for the front pant leg up to you. Then measure off and draw on both the front and

Fig. 4-6. The insets on these ecru-colored slacks feature the same print as the blouse worn with them. You could also substitute a patchwork inset. (Pants shown courtesy of the Simplicity Pattern Company, © 1975; blouse shown through courtesy of the Butterick Pattern Service.)

back leg sections a diagonal line starting 1 in. above the hemline at the inner leg seamline and extending to a point at the stitching line for side seams that is 9 in. from the pant bottom (see Fig. 4-7, left). If you're a tall person, however, you might like to make a wider inset. Cut the pattern sections apart on the diagonal line (see Fig. 4-7, right). Pin the pant legs to the fabric but remember to add ⅝ in. at the diagonal line for the seam allowance. Pin the inset pattern section to the contrasting fabric, again adding the ⅝ in. seam allowance along the diagonal line.

Cut the pieces out, and pin the insets to the pant leg sections. Make certain that you join the inset fronts to the pant fronts and the back insets to the pant backs because there is usually a difference in width between the two. Notice how points of the fabric protrude at both sides where the inset joins the pant legs (see Fig. 4-7, center). When the inset is turned down, however, the sides of the pant legs should line up with the sides of the insets. Stitch the seam, press the seam down, and then follow the pattern instructions to finish the pants. The tops of the insets should come to a point at the outer leg seams when the front and back sections are joined.

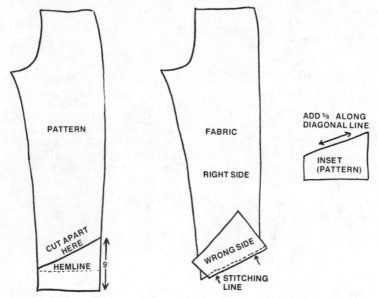

Fig. 4-7. How to cut a pattern apart to allow for the inset is shown at the left. The diagonal line ends at the side seam approximately 9 in. from the bottom of the pant leg. The width of the inset should be proportional to the wearer's height. The illustration at the right shows an inset pattern. At the center is shown a method for attaching the inset. Points of fabric jut out at both sides.

If you're using a material for the inset that is lighter in weight than the pants fabric, you might want to back the inset with another material to give it the necessary body. To make the inset from patchwork, first pin and sew the patches to old sheeting or some other cotton fabric cut to the size of the inset—but including the ⅝ in. seam allowance at the top.

If you want a wardrobe that is truly unique, why not try working with contrasting fabrics, either through using patterns featuring some of the details described in this chapter or by making minor changes in other patterns that would permit the insertion of harmonizing fabrics. The results are well worth the extra effort.

How to Make a Thrifty Coat 5

The stylish coat in Fig. 5-1 is made, in patchwork design, of an outgrown raincoat and two different draperies in coordinating colors (beige, brown, yellow, and green) picked up on a bargain table for under $5. That cost plus that of my pattern, lining material, and buttons was the only money invested in a coat that has become my daughter's favorite. Her friends think it "cool," too.

With some outgrown or outdated clothing hanging in your closets, you can do the same. The first step is to make your "material." This takes some time, but there is something so satisfying about designing your own material that you will enjoy the project.

First, however, buy the pattern you will use and cut the entire coat out of old sheets. To get started making your "material," cut out a few squares and rectangles of various sizes from the discarded garments you intend to use.

Lay one of the coat fronts cut from the sheeting on a bed or floor and experiment with design by arranging the squares and rectangles on it to please your eye. To start sewing the "patches" in place, begin about midway down the coat front, placing a square or rectangle against the raw edge of the front opening and sewing all around it to hold it in place. There is no need to turn under the raw edges of this first patch piece. *Do* crease under the raw edge of the second piece, however (the edge you will stitch on). Then stitch that creased edge over one of the raw edges of the first piece. See Fig. 5-2. Crease under

Fig. 5-1. This all-weather coat was made from patches of a raincoat and draperies.

an edge of a third patch piece, and stitch that piece over one or more of the other raw edges.

Each new creased edge should cover some raw edges of previous "patches" so that, when finished, no raw edges will show. (There is no reason why you should stick to the very edges of the patch pieces, however. Sometimes, you may want to lap over quite deeply onto the previous pieces for the sake of design.) Keep going in this fashion, always with an eye to a pleasing design, until your whole front section is covered, cutting new squares and rectangles of sizes and colors needed. Do not worry about allowing the patch pieces to extend beyond the edges of your sheeting.

Now lay the other sheeting front on the bed beside the finished front and start the design of the second front so that it will harmonize with the design of the first one. When all coat sections are finished (your "material" made), lay your pattern on those sections and cut out again. Then sew your

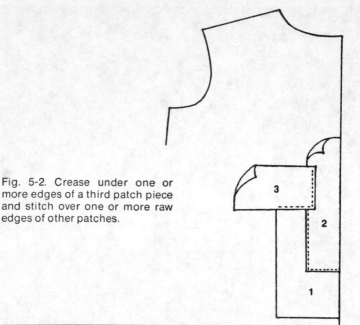

Fig. 5-2. Crease under one or more edges of a third patch piece and stitch over one or more raw edges of other patches.

Fig. 5-3. An all-weather, reversible coat. (© 1975 Simplicity Pattern Company.)

coat together according to directions, with one exception: don't bother to interface. Your coat will be firm enough because of the stitched sheet backing.

The coat pictured in Fig. 5-3 was such a satisfying project that I have already begun work on a winter coat like the one in the sketch. This coat will be made of two old coats that have hung in a closet for 10 years and two old skirts (all black and white or plain black). It will not take as much time to make as the all-weather coat because my winter coat pattern is a reversible style, which means that I will not have to make "material" for coat facings. As with the all-weather coat, again I will not have to interface because the material will be firm enough after having been sewn to the sheet backing.

I won't need to interline, either. The warmth will come from the lightweight wool material of my "patches" and from the quilted lining that I intend to use. The only cost will be for the lining material and the buttons. I can hardly wait to finish it. Try it yourself. You'll feel like an artist. And why shouldn't you? You will have designed your own coat, material and all, for only a few dollars.

Patching Up Your Gift List

Through the window by my sewing machine, a soft breeze blows and the sun comes in. I am beginning my Christmas sewing early because the gifts I am making will take an extra bit of time—they all will be made of scraps. Can you imagine?

With plenty of time to work unhurried, I can enjoy making them. There will be a vest of taffeta scraps, a baby quilt of corduroy pieces, and a baby robe of cotton scraps (see Fig. 6-1). (One year when I made one of these robes, the young mother refused to use the pretty garment as a robe but put it on the baby with her best bonnet for a Sunday coat.) There also will be a skirt, slacks, and some novelty gift items. If I have time and taffeta scraps left, I may even make myself a glamourous hostess skirt for the holidays (see Fig. 6-2).

From your own leftover sewing scraps, you can make some of the same gifts. Once you get started, you will think of other things to make—shirts, jumpers, dresses, etc. (All garments, even those of cotton, will be warm because of the backing, which can be made from old sheets.)

If you are lucky enough to live near a garment factory, as I am, you may be able to buy the scraps you need. I bought several bundles at 35¢ a pound. One pound may make several gifts, depending on size, so many beautiful things cost literally only pennies.

Directions given here are for making all the items illustrated except the clothes, for which you can use standard patterns. You probably will want to choose a simple pattern, since the scrap material you make will be the eye interest in these garments.

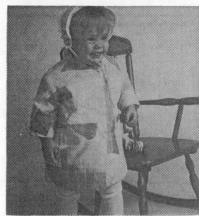

Fig. 6-1. Child's robe.

Fig. 6-2. Hostess skirt.

BASIC INSTRUCTIONS FOR MAKING MATERIAL

Measure your pattern at its widest place, and cut or tear rectangular pieces of backing to accommodate this width.

Select a scrap of pretty fabric and lay it along the edge of your backing. Machine sew the fabric scrap to the backing. Choose another piece of fabric. Lay one edge of it over the raw edge of the first piece, folding under the edge of the second piece (crease it with your fingers or press it first, if you like). Sew the folded edge of the second piece over the first. Continue adding pieces until the backing is covered and all raw edges of the scraps are covered.

You can change thread colors as you change fabric colors, or you may want to use one predominant color.

You may find it more interesting and flexible to make squares or rectangles in approximate quarter-widths of the whole pattern to be pieced together just before cutting the garment. You need not join the rectangles together in

Fig. 6-3. Slacks and skirt. (Courtesy Butterick Pattern Service.)

alignment; by shifting the alignment, you may have more flexibility in suiting the lines of the pattern.

After you have completed the rectangles, lay them out on a bed or floor. Switch them around until you find the most interesting combinations of color and design for adjacent pieces. Join the rectangles; then lay your pattern out and proceed to make the garment or item according to instructions.

SPECIAL NOTES ON GARMENTS

Some of the garments you make you may want to line to cover the seaming of the rectangles (see Fig. 6-3). The skirts and slacks shown did not require lining, but the vest and robe did (I even "patched" the lining in the robe, assembling squares of thin white material). The vest shown has an additional decorative touch—it is embroidered with a feather stitch around each scrap with two strands of embroidery floss

Fig. 6-4. Embroidered vest. (© 1975 Simplicity Pattern Company.)

51

Fig. 6-5. The wrong side of the back of the patchwork vest.

Fig. 6-6. Crib quilt.

(see Fig. 6-4). The embroidery was done after the vest was sewn together but before it was lined (see Fig. 6-5).

CRIB QUILT

The quilt in Fig. 6-6 quilt is 37 × 50 in., but you may make a smaller one by reducing the size of the blocks or by eliminating the borders around them. The quilt shown is made of corduroy, with twenty-eight 9 × 7 in. blocks (they will be 8 × 6 in. when sewn), four each of seven colors. (Each individual color will appear diagonally across the quilt.)

After cutting the 28 blocks, lay them out to arrange your color scheme. Starting on the left and working down in vertical columns the pattern scheme is (first row) red, blue, yellow, brown, gray, orange, black; (second row) black, red, blue, yellow, brown, gray, orange; (third row) orange, black, red, blue, yellow, brown, gray; (fourth row) gray, orange, black, red, blue, yellow, brown. Always start each succeeding row with the color that ended the preceding row.

The alphabet letters should be sewn on (by hand or machine) before the blocks are joined. When cutting out the letters (which may be made from the material you are using for borders), be sure to allow ¼ in. for turning under the raw edges.

For the borders and back of the quilt, select about three yards of 44 in. flannel or other material which will coordinate with the quilt blocks. Cut a piece 1½ yards long of this material for the backing. From the remaining material, cut five strips measuring 2 × 52 in.; two strips measuring 2 × 39 in.; and 24 strips, measuring 2 × 9 in. Use the shortest strips to join the blocks, following the vertical pattern described in the color arrangement. You will then have four columns, which you will join together with three 52 in. strips, adding the other two strips to the side edges. Complete the quilt top by sewing the 39 in. strips to the top and bottom edges.

With *wrong* sides together, lay the top on the back and pin in place. (If you want to use a quilt filler, insert it between the layers before pinning.) See Fig. 6-7. Trim the back so that there is a 1 in. allowance larger on all sides than the quilt top. This allowance will form the binding edge, which will be

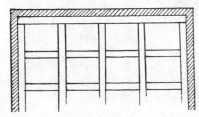

Fig. 6-7. Lay the quilt on the quilt back. Trim the back to extend 1 in. on all sides.

turned under and stitched over the quilt top. To finish the quilt, tie in the borders and corners of each block with floss or yarn. (For instructions for binding and tying, see "New Quilts from Old Blankets" Chapter 8.)

TOTE BAG

Cut two pieces of backing from firm old sheets or other suitable fabric, each 14 × 19 in. and make scrap "material." Trim the two pieces to the size above for the front and back of the tote bag. See Figs. 6-8 and 6-9. Measure down 7 in. at both sides of the two pieces, and hem those four side edges starting at the top. Make a 2½ in. machine hem at the top of each piece. About 1 in. above that, make another line of stitching. This will form a casing for the drawstrings.

Sew the front and back together, starting an inch or so below the hemline. Make two drawstrings of material, firm tape, 34 in. shoelaces, or strong cord. Thread one drawstring through the entire casing, front and back, and tie the ends together. Do the same with the other drawstring, starting from

Fig. 6-8. Front view of tote.

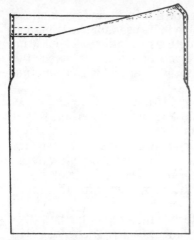

Fig. 6-9. Measure down 7 in. at both sides of the front and back of the tote. Hem the four edges.

the opposite side. Knot the ends. Close by pulling from both sides.

CLOTHESPIN BAG

To make a clothespin bag as shown in Fig. 6-10, cut backing into four pieces, each 20 × 9 in. Sew two of the pieces

Fig. 6-10. A clothespin bag.

together, seaming the long side for the front and back of the clothespin bag. Lay out the section to be used for the front and trace a circle (using a small plate as a pattern) about 3 in. below the top and equidistant from both sides. Cut out the circle, and bind the opening with bias tape of a coordinating color.

Now cut a 12 in. square of an attractive fabric and press under ½ in. on all four edges. Lay the back section out, wrong side up, and place the square on it, positioning it 2 in. down from the top and equidistant from each side. (This square serves as a shield lining to cover the backing from view at the opening.) Sew the square to the wrong side of the back piece, using a bobbin thread that will harmonize with the scrap materials of the other side.

Mark off a 3 in. length, centered at the top of the bag (this will become the opening for the hanger hook). Then mark off 2 in. on each side (see Fig. 6-11). Draw slanting lines from these marks to the opening marks at the top. Seam the back and front sections, right sides together, sewing along the marked lines at the top. Trim, turn, and press. Bind or hem the top opening.

FLOOR PILLOWS

The pillow forms shown in Fig. 6-12 are cut or molded foam rubber. For the top section of the pillow, measure the top of the foam rubber and add ⅝ in. for seam allowance all around. If you wish to make a self-cording from the scrap material, make a 2 ½ in. seam allowance instead, and this will allow enough to wrap and sew around cording. For the middle section, measure the thickness and circumference of the pillow, adding the ⅝ in. seam allowance. Cut a strip from a heavy matching material and seam it to the top section. (You

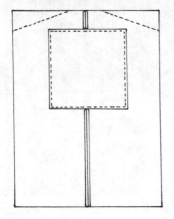

Fig. 6-11. Sew on a slant to make "shoulders" at the top of your clothespin bag.

Fig. 6-12. Floor pillows.

may insert a zipper at the seam or in the middle of the strip.) Cut the pillow bottom out of the heavy material the same size as the bottom plus ⅝ in. seam allowance all around. Seam it to the middle section. If you don't use a zipper, leave open part of the seam until the foam rubber is inserted; hand stitch to close.

CLOWN DOLL AND PILLOW TOP

The clown doll shown in Fig. 6-13 is made of circles of three sizes cut from scraps. Cut twenty-four 2½ in. circles, twenty-eight 3¼ in. circles, and twelve 4½ in. circles. These will make the doll's arms, legs, and body. For the head, cut a 6½ in. circle from white material. For the hat, cut a triangle 5½ in. on two sides, 7 in. on the other.

Using doubled thread, run a gathering stitch ⅛ in. from the edge of each circle and draw it up tightly. Flatten out the resulting pouf, and fasten the thread.

When all the circles are done, string them together with strong thread. The large circles will make the body, the medium circles will make the legs (14 circles for each) and the small circles will make the arms (12 circles for each). Attach the arms to the body at the second circle from the top of the body section; attach the legs to the bottom circle of the body. Stuff the 6½ in. circle with cotton and embroider a face on it. Attach it to the body. Make the hat by seaming the short sides of the triangle together. Hem the long side. Tack it onto the head. Sew a bell at the end of each arm and leg and at the point

Fig. 6-13. Clown doll and pillow.

of the hat. Make a ruff by gathering a strip of nylon netting
(4 × 18 in. folded lengthwise). Attach the ruff to the head.
Attach the head to the body.

The pillow top is made with the same type of poufs, except
that the raw edges of the circles are turned under before
gathering. (The circles are laid gathered side up.) To make a
pillow top about 14 in. square, you will need one hundred 3¼ in.
circles. When they are made, attach them with the sides
touching in rows of ten. Attach them to a pillow top of
contrasting color. Sew the top to the case by hand, letting the
edges of the circles extend over the edge of case. Make or buy
a pillow to fit.

Partial Patchwork and Other Tricky Techniques

As you saw in Chapter 4, patchwork can be used as a decorative feature of the garment and need not always be used to sew the whole thing. I call this technique *partial patchwork*. This chapter will show how patchwork can be used to form the front panel of a skirt or to make the main sections of a purse. Also included in this chapter are other little sewing tricks such as trimming the front panel of a skirt with velvet ribbon for a festive look, a shortcut method to help you in making things from patchwork, plus some helpful hints for combining fabrics patchwork style.

Patchwork is usually associated with everyday wear, but it can be used in sewing garments for dressy occasions too. The style of pattern you choose and the fabric used to cut the patches make all the difference. Of course, if the patchwork makes up only a part of the garment, the remainder of the fabric used will also determine whether the garment made from it will be worn as sportswear or for dressup affairs.

When looking for fabrics to go into your patchwork, don't leave any stone unturned. Like-new napkins (hopefully they're permanent press) stored away in your linen closet or material cut from garments no longer in style, provided of course the fabric isn't faded or in poor condition, could provide you with just the right shade to complement the other materials you plan to use in your patchwork. The results of making use of fabrics from a variety of sources are seen in the skirt pictured in Fig. 7-1. To make the patchwork featured in the front panel, I used an embroidered eyelet fabric cut from a seldom worn dressy maternity top along with some crisp eyelet-trimmed material taken from the bodice of an out-of-style dress. A black wool remnant was used to make the back and sides of the skirt.

Fig. 7-1. Notice the placement of the scalloped eyelet fabric at the hemline. First decide where the hemline will be and then pin the eyelet fabric on the sheeting in such a way that scallops fall at the hemline. (© 1975 Simplicity Pattern Company.)

The skirt features a front panel—a style that can be used in a variety of ways, as you'll see in this chapter. For the front panel I chose, in addition to the eyelet materials, embossed white cotton, a dainty black, white, and salmon colored print, and scraps of a solid salmon color. Because I planned to use the scalloping on the eyelet fabrics at the hemline of the patchwork panel, I first figured out by holding the pattern up to me just where the hemline should be. Then, using the pattern section for the front panel, I cut out the panel from old sheeting, making it as long as needed but including the hem allowance.

Next I went to work pinning the patches (see the directions in Chapter 6) on the sheeting, arranging them so that the scalloping on the eyelets fell at the hemline and in other positions where they would show up to best advantage. I also patched the front panel below the eyelet border, although this part would later be turned under to form the hem. I stitched the top edges of this last row of patches but did not stitch down the scallops at the hemline because I didn't want them turned into the hem, thus losing the effect I was trying to achieve. I made certain, too, that no raw edges would be exposed at the hemline of the panel section when it was time to hem the skirt. In hemming the skirt, I did the front panel first and then went on to do the sides and back. The finished skirt with its lovely scalloped hemline, when topped with a frilly blouse, was perfect for dress occasions.

You can take the same skirt pattern and make it up in the long version, too. If your pattern does not include the ankle-length style, you can still use this particular pattern by adding to the length. Determine the proper length to make the skirt by measuring it against a long skirt or dress pattern of another style. When lengthening the pattern, though, curve the hemline to make it exactly as it was originally in the short version.

The pattern for the festive holiday skirt shown at the left in Fig. 7-2 was lengthened in this manner. However, you must be certain that the skirt will be wide enough at the bottom to permit you to move about freely. The skirt fabric, a remnant in a dark green print bought at an after-Christmas sale the previous year, featured rich shades of gold, red, and blue and proved ideal for holiday wear. To emphasize both the design and the colors, I trimmed the front panel of the skirt with velveteen ribbon. In doing this I let the block design in the fabric serve as a guide to placement of the ribbon. I was able to achieve a mitered effect by folding the ribbon at the corners of the rectangles. The raw ends of the ribbon that were not hidden in the seam were turned under and stitched.

Shown at the right in Fig. 7-2 is the same style made up for summer wear as a patio skirt. However, the striped seersucker which featured different designs in each stripe was so attractive that I felt it would show off to better advantage if

Fig. 7-2. The long skirt at the left is sewn in a Christmas-like print and color featuring a front panel trimmed with blue and green velvet ribbon. The trimming was done to emphasize parts of the design. The front panel of the summery print skirt at the right was cut with the print running horizontally. The remaining skirt sections were cut with the print running up and down. The seams of the front panel were rickrack-trimmed for emphasis. (© 1975 Simplicity Pattern Company.)

used crosswise rather then lengthwise in the front panel. To further the resultant apron effect, I sewed rickrack, in a shade that picked up one of the colors in the print, over the seams of the front panel. Since the stripes were placed vertically at the sides and back of the skirt, I avoided a roly-poly look that I might have had if the stripes had run horizontally around the entire skirt. I don't recall if there was any advantage to this as far as fabric savings were concerned, but I do know that there was enough of the seersucker left to make a midriff that came out of the dryer crisp and wrinkle-free. Hint: It's a good idea to try to find a use for the leftover scraps right after you're through working with the fabric instead of storing them away where you're apt to forget about them.

By using a skirt pattern calling for a front panel that ends in a pleat on each side and simpler fabrics, it is possible to obtain a sportier look. A purchased navy cotton remnant provided just enough fabric for the back, side panels, and the waistband of the skirt shown in Fig. 7-3. Unlike the other skirt, which featured a front panel and side and back sections cut in one piece that were joined in a center back seam, this pattern called for separate side front and back sections with both side and center back seams. I used a red, white, and blue color scheme for the patchwork panel and, since the skirt was designed for casual wear rather than for dress, I used gay

Fig. 7-3. This sporty version of the patchwork-trimmed skirt features a pleat on each side of the front panel. (© 1975 Simplicity Pattern Company.)

prints in the patchwork that were cut from fabrics such as cottons, cotton blends, and lightweight denims.

When making your patchwork, you can minimize a predominant color or print by using fewer and smaller pieces of that particular fabric and also by placing the more outstanding patches under rather than on top of the other less vivid hues and prints. The patches that overlap the others usually catch the eye first. When working with a heavy or extremely bulky material, though, such as fake fur, it's best not to place any patches on top of it but rather to place it in a position where it overlaps its neighbors.

Sometimes you might find the perfect color match for the other materials you've collected to make a patchwork item, but the fabric may not be suitable otherwise in that it is too dressy or too sporty to combine with the other fabrics. For instance, if your patchwork will be composed entirely of tweeds, solid colors of wool, and wool or wool blend plaids, you will not want to interject swatches of cotton or crepe even if the color is just right. A color match in itself does not insure complete success in matching fabrics. But don't be afraid to try combinations of figured fabrics in patchwork such as miniprints, polka dots, and gingham checks, provided both the colors and materials are in harmony with each other. Simply insert patches of coordinating solid colors here and there to avoid a cluttered look in the patchwork.

In creating a patchwork panel or fabric, you might want to take a shortcut by pinning the pattern pieces to be made from patchwork on old sheeting or some other lightweight cotton material and cutting them out. Then pin the patches directly to the pattern pieces that you cut from the sheeting. That way you won't see any of your patchwork going to waste.

You can take this shortcut to sew the roomy indispensable purses shown in Fig. 7-4. Although I started out by sewing them entirely from patchwork, by the time I made the second or third one I devised some shortcuts. While they didn't detract from the appearance of the finished product, they did save me considerable time. The first time around I took the time to patch not only the long skinny straps on the purse but also the inner compartment of an outside pocket which didn't show anyway. Patching the narrow strap sections proved to be a mistake, though, because this made the straps bulky and extremely difficult to turn right side out. When making the next purses, therefore, I simply reserved the longest of the remnants I'd collected and used them to cut out the strap sections. The side and bottom sections, although cut in contrasting fabrics, were not patched either. When patching the part that would make up the pocket facing and the area that would be hidden by the pocket, I used my largest scraps or, in some cases, one large piece depending on the fabric available. All these shortcuts served to cut down on my total sewing time.

The linings for the purses also can be cut from remnants, and a regular lining fabric or a Dacron-cotton blend can be used. The lining, however, should be sewn from a fabric that can be handled for dry-cleaning or laundering purposes in exactly the same way as the outside of the purse.

To sew a patchwork purse for winter use, try using fabrics such as corduroy, fake fur, acrylics, polyesters, or wool. The one shown at the left in Fig. 7-4 features a combination of wools and acrylics, so I dry-clean it in a coin-operated machine. A gold acrylic with a woven design as well as patches of both red and green acrylic, a brown and white herringbone tweed, and a forest green wool were used to make it.

The summer version of the purse shown at the right of Fig. 7-4 is made up of embossed white cottons, pale blue and soft aqua cotton blends, white eyelet fabric, plus several miniprints in pastel colors. Because I felt that this purse was not appropriate for use after Labor Day due to the light colors in it, I stitched up another one that was entirely composed of dark cottons in both solids and prints. Both cotton purses are washable.

Another way to use patchwork would be to feature the crazy quilt, as this particular type is called, on the front of a bolero or vest and cutting the vest back from a coordinating solid color. You could also sew a cozy robe for wear in chilly weather using an all-over or partial patchwork technique.

SEWING TRICKS

Some sewing tricks, such as the placement of certain details like patch pockets, front bands, or yokes on the bias of the fabric, can be copied from the manufacturers of ready-to-wear items. Other tricks you'll pick up on your own as you continue to sew. Cutting one or two small parts of a garment on the bias, however, can be very effective, particularly when working with stripes, plaids, and certain types of prints.

Look to ready-to-wear too for topstitching tricks. For instance, topstitching can be used not only to liven up a solid color dress but also to coordinate a two-piece outfit. If you're sewing a pair of white slacks to wear with a halter in a yellow, white, and black print, you could topstitch the waistband of the pants in either yellow or black. You might even want to use one

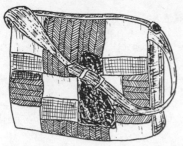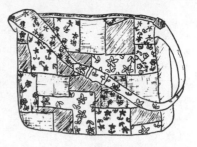

Fig. 7-4. The illustration at the left shows the winter version of a patchwork purse done in a variety of wool and fake fur fabrics. At the right is a summer version featuring floral prints and pastel colors. (Courtesy the McCall Pattern Company.)

of those colors of thread to sew the zipper in place, but only if you can sew a nice straight seam. A white skirt intended for wear with both a pink top and a baby blue one could be topstitched at the waistband in both those shades with one color at the top and the other at the bottom edge. Of course this does put a limit on the amount of mixing and matching you can do in that you wouldn't want to team a skirt or slacks that is topstitched in pink and blue with a yellow or brown blouse. But if you plan to wear a skirt or slacks with only one or two tops, why not topstitch the waistbands in shades to match for a truly coordinated look that will cost you nothing to achieve?

If you now prefer bodysuits to blouses but still have a couple of perfectly good blouses hanging in your closet, you might want to convert them into bodysuits. You can do this by the addition of a knit panty which has a snap opening in the crotch. Of course these bottoms can be bought and attached, but since they're relatively easy to sew and can be made from leftover knits (not bonded ones), you might like to stitch up your own. Use a pair of panties or a bathing suit bottom to guide you in making a tissue paper pattern, but remember to allow for the seam at the top, sides, legs, and crotch and for overlapping the front and back sections slightly at the crotch opening. If the blouse is cut rather full at the sides, you might want to take it in somewhat if you can do so without making the blouse too tight. Bodysuits are usually cut without the extra fullness that a blouse has.

Then, too, if the blouse has a front or back button opening that extends the length of the blouse, close the last button on it before attaching the panty and stitch across the bottom edges of the opening. After cutting the panty out, seam the front and back sections together, keeping the right sides of each facing inside. Turn under the edges of the pant legs in a ½ in. seam to form a casing for the elastic. Use a safety pin to thread narrow elastic through the casing. Stitch the elastic in place at the point of entry before pulling it all the way through and again at the opposite end of the casing.

Turn the front edge of the crotch opening to the inside in a $3/8$ in. hem and stitch. Turn back the edge of the crotch opening to the outside in a $5/8$ in. hem and stitch. Sew twill or bias tape over the hems. Sew snaps in place on the tape with the ball part of the snap on the front section of the crotch and the socket part on the back.

Keeping the right sides together, pin the top of the panty to the bottom of the blouse and try on your bodysuit. If the panty is too long, cut it away at the top. Then seam the panty to the blouse.

In some instances leftover pieces of fabric are so small or narrow that there doesn't seem to be any use for them. However, sometimes you can double the width of your scrap pieces by placing your pattern pieces nearer to the selvedges and away from the fold if the width of the material will permit this. Then, due to the fact that the leftover fabric lies along the fold, you'll end up with larger pieces than you would have otherwise.

To sum up, patchwork and some of the other techniques demonstrated in this chapter can enable you to stitch up new additions to your wardrobe without putting a dent in your budget and also to remodel or recycle items you no longer wear. You might find, too, that you prefer the original clothes you sew from remnants to those garments sewn from fabrics bought expressly to use with a particular pattern. Meanwhile, you can have fun turning the findings in your rag bag into glad rags; you reap compliments, and you save money. What more could you ask for?

Scraps Can
Save You Money

Vests, hats, halters, and baby bibs are but a few of the items you can sew from pieces of fabric seemingly too small for any use. A glance at the pattern books, particularly in the children's and bazaar sections, will yield a wealth of articles that can be sewn from scraps. If you make some of these things from scraps you will not only gain some additions to your wardrobe or some other handy items at no cost to you, but you'll also have the satisfaction of knowing that they were sewn from a piece of fabric that was originally thought to be useless because of its small size.

It only takes a fraction of a yard to sew a midriff like the one pictured at the left in Fig. 8-1, and it is even possible to use different fabrics for the front and back sections if you don't have enough of one kind to sew the entire top. If you find that you can't cut the back section in one piece as the pattern directs, cut it from two pieces instead and add ⅝ in. for the seam allowance at the center back. That way you won't have to place that piece on the fold of the material.

A halter like the one at the right in Fig. 8-1 lends itself to being made from short pieces of coordinating fabrics because it is composed of several pattern pieces. Four fabrics were used in sewing the halter, although only three are visible. A scrap of leftover eyelet provided the fabric for the collar, while the undercollar, facings and lining were all cut from a white Dacron-cotton blend. A predominantly yellow print with a hint of white and black in it was used in the bodice; the midriff section was sewn from a bold black and white print. Both the yellow and the black fabrics were used to make the duster shown in Chapter 2.

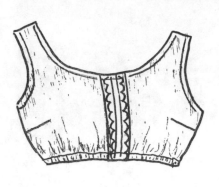

Fig. 8-1. Midriffs and halters take little material; therefore, they're ideal for using up your remnants. The midriff shown could be sewn from one or two fabrics. The halter was made from four fabrics and features an eyelet collar, two different prints, and a plain white undercollar and lining. (Midriff © 1975 Simplicity Pattern Company, halter courtesy Butterick Pattern Service.)

Because a simple midriff or halter like those described above takes so little fabric to make, you can usually find material in your collection of remnants for use in sewing one up. Lightweight seersuckers, piques, knits, cottons, and cotton blends can be used to stitch up cool summer tops.

Styled like vests, the tops pictured in Fig. 8-2 call for only a small amount of material. The vests can be worn with or

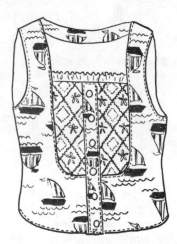

Fig. 8-2. The vest at the left features an eyelet inset. At the right is shown the same vest sewn in two coordinating prints. A common factor in both prints is the yellow, white, and black color scheme. (Courtesy of the McCall Pattern Company.)

without a blouse under them. The vest at the left is sewn up in a white Dacron-cotton blend and features a contrasting eyelet inset. The vest at the right is made from a black and yellow sailboat print having a white background. The yellow contrasting inset, cut from a remnant, has white and black in the design and coordinates well with the sailboat print. The white vest could be teamed with pants or a skirt of almost any color, while the vest made from the print fabric could be worn with pants in a color that matches one of those in the top.

You can use up your remnants, too, by combining two different but harmonious fabrics to make a pair of shorts. This can be done in two ways. For instance, you can cut the front sections from a print fabric and the back pieces from a shade that picks up one of the colors of the print. Or you can cut the right front and left back of the shorts from one fabric and the left front and right back sections from a coordinating one. When made in this fashion, shorts require very little of each fabric.

Hats are another item that can be sewn from scraps, particularly if they are of the six-section variety. By cutting each petal shape in the crown from a different lightweight fabric, you can sew an eye-catching beach hat using a pattern that calls for a brim. Eyelets, piques, ginghams, cottons, and cotton blends are some of the fabrics that could be used. Coordinate the colors as you would when working with patchwork. The colorful jockey hat shown in Fig. 8-3 can be made in much the same way. Featuring ties which can be tucked into the crown, the hat is intended for wear as a rain hat and will protect your hairdo from the rain and mist or will serve as a coverup for hair in need of a set.

You can make a furry hat using a hat pattern with a six-section crown. The beige hat in Fig. 8-4 has a peak and ties

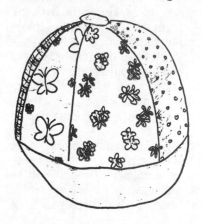

Fig. 8-3. Rain hat sewn from colorful scraps of cotton has ties which can be tucked inside.

Fig. 8-4. This fake fur features a peak and ties sewn from brown double knit. Suede cutouts (these came in a package) trim three of the hat sections.

sewn from a brown knit fabric. (Hint: the seams will barely show on a fur fabric if you use a straight pin to free the hairs from the seam.) Three of the crown sections in the hat are decorated with suede cutouts in varying shades of brown. Hats for winter wear also can be made from woolens, corduroys, and quilted fabrics. If you're planning to attach ties to your hat, sew both the ties and the peak in the same fabric, preferably an unbonded knit. And you'll have a unique outfit for blustery days if you make or trim your hat in the same fabric you used to sew a pair of slacks.

Although the sectioned hats crop up in pattern catalogs from time to time with slight variations, rarely do the hats call for ties; therefore, I'm including my own pattern for them. However, you might have to make some adjustments to the pattern in order for the ties to be fitted to different styles of hats. Your best bet would be to shop for a pattern having lines similar to the hat in the illustration. Also, to avoid wasting your fabric, make up the ties from a piece of scrap material first. Then you can determine what alterations, if any, will be needed.

To make the ties, start by ruling off brown wrapping paper into 1 in squares and copying the pattern in the squares (see Fig. 8-5.) If you number the rows of squares first, it will be easier to do. Cut out the pattern, and use it to make two sets of ties (one for the facing), or four pieces in all. All seams will be

^{1}₂ in. in these instructions. Seam the center backs of each set together. Press the seams open. Then, keeping right sides together, pin the ties to the tie facing, leaving the top edges open for turning. Stitch. Trim the seams and the ends of the ties; clip the curved edges. Turn the ties right side out and press. Baste the raw edges together. Pin the ties to the bottom edges of the hat, on the outside, matching the center backs of both the hat and the ties and stitch. (Attach the ties before sewing on hatband but after attaching the peak.)

There's nothing like a head scarf to protect your hair from the devastating effects of the summer sun or to hide your hair after a dip. A simple lined one you can make which can be tied under the chin or in the back is described in the following text. You might want to sew several in fabrics to match all your sportswear outfits.

To make the scarf, you will need to cut out two 15 × 15 × 20-in. triangles. Cut two 16 in. pieces of bias tape for the ties. Fold the tape in half, keeping the edges even, and

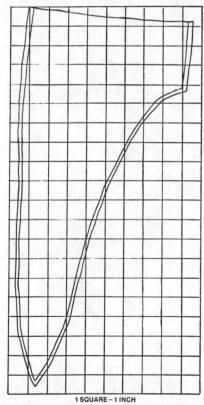

Fig. 8-5. For your convenience, pattern for ties is given in small and average sizes.

1 SQUARE – 1 INCH

71

stitch close to the edge. If you're working with double-fold tape, you won't have to fold it in half as this will have already been done for you. Pin the ties in place on both sides, ½ in. away from the front edge, positioning them so that they extend almost to the opposite side of the scarf. Machine baste the ties in place. With the right sides together and the ties sandwiched between them, pin the lining to the scarf. Stitch ½ in. away from the edges, leaving an opening for turning and taking care not to catch the free ends of the ties in the seams. Trim the seam and corners. Turn the scarf right side out and slip stitch the opening closed and press.

Perky glass cases also can be sewn from leftover pieces of fabric. Use quilted cotton material or felt cut from squares (available in variety stores) to make them.

For the "winking eye" case shown in Fig. 8-6 you will need two 3½ × 6 in. rectangles of felt. Use the pattern in Fig. 8-7 to make a pair of glasses from felt of a contrasting color. Glue the glasses to one of the rectangles. Draw the eye on the felt and embroider it, following the key. Glue bits of fringe above the embroidered eye to form the lashes. Trim and thin out another piece of fringe for the eyelash of the winking eye. Glue in place. Cut a piece of baby rickrack for the eyelid, and glue it in a curved position above the fringed lashes. Stitch the front and back sections together, keeping the right sides facing out.

To make the quilted case in Fig. 8-8 cut out two rectangles in the 3½ × 6 in. size. Bind one 3½ in. side on each rectangle. This will be the top of the case when it's completed. Pin the rectangles together with the right sides on the inside and stitch, leaving the bound edge open. Turn the case right side out.

A comb case, too, can be made from felt. The mouse-decorated one in Fig. 8-9 makes a nice stocking stuffer

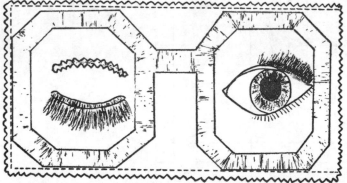

Fig. 8-6. Winking eyeglass case made from felt squares or scraps.

DRAPERY FRINGE

BLACK SATIN STITCH

BLUE SATIN STITCH

USE BLACK THREAD TO EMBROIDER
REMAINDER IN OUTLINE STITCH.

1 SQUARE = 1 IN.

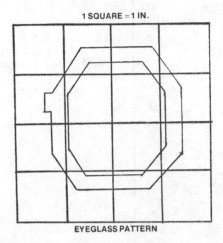

EYEGLASS PATTERN

Fig. 8-7. Follow the key given at the top to embroider the eye. The eyeglass pattern is shown at the bottom. Mark off your paper into 1 in. squares; then copy the glass frame in the squares.

with a comb tucked in it and could help encourage a youngster to develop good grooming habits. To make the case you'll need felt squares or scraps in contrasting colors.

Use a pinking or scalloping shears to cut two 2¼ × 5½ in. rectangles from the felt. Enlarge the mouse pattern by drawing 1 in. squares on a piece of paper and copying the mouse square by square. (See Fig. 8-10.) Cut out the mouse and trace around it on a contrasting color of felt. Cut out the felt mouse, center it on one of the felt rectangles, and hand sew or glue it in place. Use a paper punch to make felt dots for the eyes and nose. Cut the whiskers from black felt. Sew or glue the features in place on the mouse. With the right sides facing out, sew the front and back of the case together.

Colorful patches for children's clothes or for your jeans can be cut from fabrics having geometric or other designs or from solid shades. You save because you don't have to buy the iron-on kind. First decide what part of the motif you want to use, and then cut the patch slightly bigger than the desired size. Turn under the raw edges and stitch. Then pin the patch

Fig. 8-8. A flower print glass case sewn from a scrap of quilted fabric.

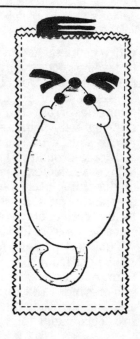

Fig. 8-9. This easy-to-make comb case is sewn from scraps of felt.

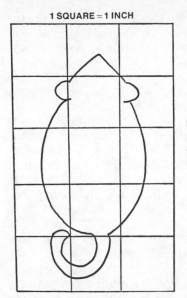

Fig. 8-10. To make the mouse, rule off paper into 1 in. squares and copy the pattern in the blocks.

over the worn area and sew in place. When patching clothes, for best results try to use fabrics from the same family as the garment to be patched. The colors don't necessarily have to match; in fact, kids generally like the wilder combinations.

Small pieces of fabric in a matching color also can be used to face a garment when you're running short of material. Then, too, if only a partial lining is called for you might be able to use leftover fabric rather than a specially purchased one.

Unusual coasters can be made from scraps of cotton quilted fabric (not the puffy kind), as shown in Fig. 8-11. For

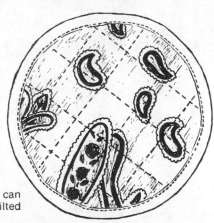

Fig. 8-11. Unusual coasters can be sewn from circles of quilted cotton fabric.

each one you want to make, cut out two 3½ in. circles from the quilted material. Pin them together with the right sides out, and stitch close to the edges. Bind with bias tape. A set of these would make a nice gift.

If you have any marble enthusiasts in the family, you might want to turn leftover pieces of sturdy cotton into handy marble bags for them. Here's how it's done.

Cut two rectangles from the fabric, measuring 8 in. long and 10 in. wide. Seam the two together at the sides and the bottom, with the wrong sides facing out. Turn to the right side. At both side seams, make small buttonholes starting exactly 1 in. from the top edge. Turn under ¼ in. at the top and stitch. Then turn under a second time to form a ¾ in. casing. The buttonholes should now be at the top of the bag. Stitch close to the edge of the casing.

To make the drawstrings, cut two 28 in. pieces of bias tape. Fold each in half, and stitch close to the edges. Use a safety pin to thread one of the drawstrings through the casing, starting and ending at the same buttonhole. Then insert the remaining drawstring in the opposite buttonhole. Thread through the casing, and bring the drawstring out through the same opening. Seam the ends of the tape together, and work the drawstrings until the seamed parts are hidden in the casing.

Babies, too, can benefit from fabric scraps. For instance, you can make all kinds of bibs for them, including plastic-lined

Fig. 8-12. Dressup bib for a baby who's going places.

ones, teething bibs, and show-off types for special occasions. Made to resemble a vest, the bib shown in Fig. 8-12 is fast and easy to sew up because the details on it are drawn on with permanent marking pens rather than embroidered.

Start by cutting out two pieces of fabric shaped as shown. With the right sides together, stitch around the sides and bottom, leaving the neck edges open for turning. Trim the seam; clip the curves and close the seam at the center front between the points. Turn the bib right side out and press. Machine baste the neck edges together. Bind the neck edges, allowing extra tape for the ties. Copy the details on the bib using permanent marking pens.

Only a small amount of a firmly woven fabric is needed to make a handsome litterbag for your car. If you're short on one kind of fabric, you can sew it from two leftover pieces and still end up with an attractive and useful car accessory. The one shown in Fig. 8-13 was made from a heavy seersucker material featuring 1 in. black and white checks and was bound with a turquoise binding.

The bag is made up of three sections: front, back, and back facing. The facing, I feel, serves as a reinforcement in the buttonhole area. To make the bag, cut one piece for the back shaped as shown, measuring 13½ in. at its longest point and 8½ in. wide. The sides measure 10 in. in length with the curved top section taking up the remainder. The back facing is shaped like the back but is shorter in length, measuring 7 in. from the center top to the bottom. The front section measures 10 in. in length and 8½ in. in width. All seams are ½ in. throughout these instructions and are sewn on the right side.

Turn under ½ in. at the bottom edge of the facing section and stitch. Finish one 8½ in. wide side of the front section by sewing the seam binding to the edge. Make a 1 in. hem in the side you finished with binding, and sew by hand or machine.

Pin the facing to the back of the bag, matching the outer edges and keeping the wrong sides together; stitch. Pin the front section of the bag to the back with the wrong sides facing inside and stitch. Trim the seams to ¼ in., clip the curves, and round off the corners. Bind the edges of the top and bottom sections of the bag in one continuous motion.

Now obviously you'll need some sort of opening at the top so that you can suspend the bag from a knob on the dashboard. If this knob is a small one, you might be able to get away with a buttonhole of the size needed. But if you need a larger opening than a buttonhole would provide, draw a circle of the desired size in the center of the curved top section. Set your machine for a buttonhole stitch. I set my stitch length between 0 and 1

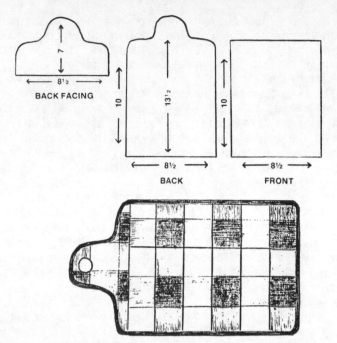

BACK FACING

7

8½

10

13½

10

8½

BACK

8½

FRONT

Fig. 8-13. Black and white checked litterbag makes a handsome and handy car accessory.

and my zigzag at 3 and found that this gave me the size stitch I wanted. You'll have to experiment with your machine until you come up with the right combination. Stitch around the circle you drew, then cut away the material in the center, cutting as close as possible to the stitching. After this step, I stitched around the opening a second time to overcast all the raw edges.

Fabric scraps can be put to use making children's clothes and appliques for them, bazaar items, doll clothes, and aprons. So with these things in mind, start saving your scraps, sew them up, and see your savings mount.

Leather Stitchery

Since leather clothing and accessories are now so fashionable (but expensive), you may have asked yourself whether it might be possible to make them. It is.

I have found leather pieces in half a dozen different colors at mill-end and factory outlets, and perhaps by this time they may be found in fabric houses as well. If not, whatever you can make from leather you can make from vinyl, suede cloth, and the fake fur fabrics.

Leather makes glamorous gifts, and here are a few of the things that you can make easily and, in most cases, rather quickly. Instructions are given for making the accessories and the pillow. For the garments, you should use a *simple* pattern of your own choice. I stress the word "simple" because, for these garments, the eye appeal is in the material.

SKIRT

The leather skirt shown in Fig. 9-1 has no seams in the front or back. It has no waistband either and is finished with wide bias tape, faced to eliminate the raw edges of the tape. (Cut two strips of tape and face them.) Cut a piece of the faced bias tape the length of the waistline, plus 2 in. for turning under at the ends. Place the tape against the right side of the skirt edge to cover the raw edge for about ½ in. (In other words, your tape will lap the skirt edge to make an extension at the top of the skirt.) Topstitch very close to the edge of the tape. After stitching, turn the tape to the inside of the skirt and secure it by tacking at the side seams to prevent rolling out. (See Chapter 13.)

The zipper at the left side is inserted according to the usual instructions. However, if your leather should be too thick for

Fig. 9-1. Leather skirts. (Courtesy Butterick Pattern Service.)

folding over in the regular way, trim away a bit more than the seam allowance for the length of the metal part of the zipper, lay this very narrow rectangular opening you have just made on top of the zipper, and sew all around so that the raw edges of the leather "frame" the zipper. Finish the bottom of the skirt with a fringe (about 3 in. deep by ½ in. wide) or with a facing. To face the bottom, cut two leather strips ½ in. wide and the width of the front and back of the skirt bottom. Sew the strips to the skirt bottom, wrong sides together stitching close to the edge. Stitch again on the opposite side of the facing. (The raw edge of the skirt is not turned under. The double-stitched facing finishes it, see Fig. 9-2.)

TRIM

To trim a fabric skirt with a 2½ in. leather band, cut the skirt 2½ in. shorter than the desired length. Then cut the

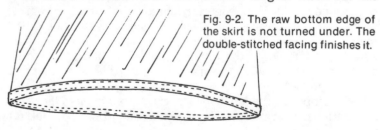

Fig. 9-2. The raw bottom edge of the skirt is not turned under. The double-stitched facing finishes it.

pieces of leather (mine matched the color of the skirt fabric) the length of the front and back skirt bottoms and 3½ in. wide. With a ½ in. seam, sew the leather pieces to the skirt front and back. Seam the sides. Bind the leather bottom of the skirt with bias strips of skirt fabric cut 2½ in. wide. Sew to the wrong side first then top stitch on the right side.

JUMPER

The ideal jumper pattern will have no front or back seams and will have a neck big enough to slip over the head. If the neck is not big enough, cut a very narrow rectangle in the middle of the back of the neck and "frame" a little zipper as was done at the side seam of the skirt. Or make a neck closing this way: slit the back of the neck as far as needed to go over the head. On the left side of the slit, sew a leather extension 1½ in. wide and 1 in. longer than the measurement of the slit. Apply self-adhering tape to the extension and to the underside of the right side of the slit. All the edges will remain raw. Finish the armholes, neck edges, and bottom of the garment by trimming off the seam allowances and facing as for the leather skirt.

Fig. 9-3. Jumper, right, and vest, left, for children.

CHILD'S VEST

You can finish this by facing, or you can line it if you like. (See Fig. 9-3, left.) Make the lining a little bigger than the vest because leather has a tendency to stretch. Place the lining on the vest, right sides together, and stitch all around, leaving an opening at the bottom for turning. Turn and crease under the seam allowances of the opening. Then topstitch close to the edge of the garment all around, closing the opening as you stitch. Make another row of stitching about ¼ in. from the first row. Finish the armholes by cutting facing strips and applying them this way: Make your first row of stitching close to the edge. Now—when making your second row of stitching—catch in the armhole lining all around. (If you prefer, you can line the whole vest this way by laying the lining inside the vest, wrong sides together, and catching the lining under the facing when stitching the facing the second time.)

Perhaps you'd like to try your hand at a patchwork vest. For a child, cut blocks 4 × 2¾ in. of one color or several and sew, long sides together. For a lady's vest, cut blocks 5¼ × 3¼ in. When cutting out, lay the pattern at the bottom of your block "material" so that any partial blocks will come at the shoulder.

FRINGED BAG

To make a fringed bag as shown in Fig. 9-4, make a paper pattern 18 in. long by 11 in. wide. This will be the back and the front flap of your bag in one piece. Make another pattern 11 × 11 in. This will be the front of the bag. Cut a pattern for the fringe 9 × 10 in. Lay patterns on leather and cut out the three pieces.

Place the fringe piece (9 × 10 in.) on the bottom edge of the back piece, wrong side of fringe to right side of back. Sew so that ½ in. will be leftover on either side of the back piece. Because leather has a tendency to stretch, start at the middle and sew to each side.

At the top of the front piece, turn a 2 in. "hem" to the wrong side and tape it in place with a bit of cellophane tape. (You will not hem this turned-down piece; it will be held in place by the side seams.) Now place the front of the bag on the back of the bag, right sides together, and seam at bottom and sides with ½ in. seams, with the fringe inside of the bag and kept out of the way of seaming. (Start from the bottom center and sew across and then up the side. Sew the other half.)

Remove the tape from the "hem," and turn the bag right side out. Trim the seam allowance from the rest of the bag to form the flap.

Fig. 9-4. Fringed bag.

Lay the fringe piece out flat and, with a pencil, mark off the fringes. Do not make them narrower than ¼ in. in width as they may tear off with use. When cutting the fringing, stop ½ in. from the bottom of the bag. Fringe the flap to a depth of about 3½ in.

For the shoulder strap, cut a strip of leather 2½ × 32 in. Fold it lengthwise so that one raw edge laps the other raw edge. Have the lap close to the edge of the strap and stitch along that edge. Then make another stitching along the opposite edge to match. Attach the strap at the side seams of the bag with the lap side down. No need to turn under the raw ends of the strap. (If your leather is thick, cut the strap 1½ in. wide, fold it in half, and stitch down both sides, leaving the raw edge exposed.)

If you wish to round the bottom of the bag, be sure to cut the same "round" out of the top of the fringe so that the two pieces will join smoothly.

PATCHWORK BAG

This lady's bag can be made by cutting 40 blocks 4 × 2¾ in. from two or more colors or all one color. (A child's bag, finished size about 8½ × 8½ in., can be made by cutting 24 blocks of the same size.)

For a lady's bag, take 20 blocks and sew the long sides together to make four rows with five blocks in a row. Now sew three rows together to form the bottom part of the front or back of the bag. Do *not* sew on the top row of blocks yet. Put together the other 20 blocks in the same way.

Cut 20 strips of leather 4 × ½ in. Use 10 strips to face the other 10, stitching on both sides of each strip. (These faced strips will make the loops to hold the drawstring.) Fold the strips in half and sew one in the middle of each block along the top of the third row of blocks on both the front and back sections of the bag.

(If you would like to line your bag, use one of the three-row sections as a pattern and cut two pieces of lining the same width as your pattern and 1 in. longer.)

Now sew the fourth row of blocks to the other three rows so that the loops are sewn between the third and fourth rows. Sew again for strength. Sew the side seams and the bottom then sew again.

If you choose not to line your bag, you can finish it at this stage by turning under the top of it (fourth row) to the inside as far as the seam line holding the loops. Stitch the raw, turned-down edge against the bag. Make the drawstrings according to the directions that follow.

To line the bag, sew the side seams of the lining pieces but do not sew the bottom. Turn the leather bag right side out. Do *not* turn the lining. Slip the lining over the bag, right sides together and sew the lining to the bag, all around the top. Now pull out the lining and sew the open end together, turning it over twice to cover the raw edges. Push the lining down inside the bag.

For the drawstrings, cut two strips 46 in. long by 1½ in. wide (piece if necessary). Make according to the directions for the fringed bag but sew on only one side of the strip. (If the leather is thick, fold the strip in half and stitch, leaving the raw edges exposed.) Thread the strip from one side, all the way around the bag and tie it into a knot. Do the same with the other drawstring, starting from the opposite side and tie. This bag, when finished, measures about 11 × 12 in.

To make a little larger bag, cut the blocks 3¼ × 5¼ in. and join the three blocks in a row, *short* ends together. Make five rows of three blocks each. Sew together the bottom four rows, add the loops, and then sew on the top row. Finish as for the foregoing bag.

EVENING BAG

Cut 45 blocks 2 in. square. Make nine rows of blocks, five in a row, and sew the rows together.

To make the envelope part of the bag, fold up one end 4½ in., right sides together, and with ½ in. seams, seam the sides up 4 in. (leaving free ½ in. at the top edge of the envelope).

The lining will be made in two parts. For the envelope part, cut a piece of material 8 × 9 in. For the flap end of the lining, cut a piece of material 8 × 7½ in. Sew together an 8 × 9 in. lining piece, sewing the side seams up 4 in., leaving ½ in. free at the top. Join that top edge of the lining to the top edge of the bag, right sides together. Turn the lining to the inside and topstitch the edge. Sew the 8 × 7½ in. lining piece to the flap end of the bag and turn. Top stitch if leather isn't too thick.

By hand, stitch the free end of the flap lining to the free end of the envelope lining down inside the bag.

HEADBANDS

A simple headband is made by cutting a piece of leather ¾ in. wide and about 20 in. long (just shorter than head measurement). Sew 10 in. ties at either end. (If the leather is thin, face the ties for added strength.) If desired, the headband may be decorated with beads.

Another headband is made by cutting a strip 20 in. long and 1½ in. wide. Cut out diamond shapes for trimming, ¾ in. wide by 1 in. long. Sew these diamond pieces to the headband with a sewing machine. (Mark around them with a pencil first for accurate placing when sewing.) Sew colored beads around the diamond pieces. Sew ties at the back as for the foregoing headband.

BELTS

A simple belt can be made from a leather strip 2 yards by 1½ in. and fringed at the ends about 10 in.

Another attractive belt can be made from a piece of leather cut 2 in. shorter than waist measurement. Cut about 3 in. wide at the back and taper to 1½ in. at the front ends. Loop the front ends around rings (bought at a department or fabric store) and stitch the ends against the belt. Face both sides of the belt with ½ in. facing as was done for the skirt and jumper hemline. For the belt closing, cut two thongs 32 in. long by 1 in. wide. Fold over lengthwise, the wrong sides together, and stitch along both sides. Folding in half, tie the thongs to the rings at the front of the belt.

PILLOW

Cut 81 blocks 2 in. square and sew them together, alternating colors (or all one color). With ¼ in. seams, sew nine rows with nine blocks in each row.

To complete the pillowcase, cut a back for it measuring 14½ × 16 in. A good fabric for the back is a knit because it is a bit stretchy, an aid when sewing to leather. Sew a 1½ in. wide strip of that same fabric across one end of the pillow top, right sides together. (This strip will be turned under to be stitched to the 1½ in. extension on the back of the pillowcase.)

Now sew the back of the pillow to the front, right sides together, so that the long end of the pillow back extends at the same side of the pillow as the 1½ in. extension sewn to the pillow front. (Smooth out the leather front as much as possible, without stretching, while sewing to the back.) Insert the pillow in the case and close the open side by turning the front and back extensions to the inside and hand stitching them together. Tassels may be bought or made from embroidery floss.

Easy Lingerie Budget Sewing

Every week my daughter came running home from her piano lesson in a state of excitement. (About her music lesson? Hardly.) She was excited over "the beautiful clothes Betty Smith was sewing." Since Betty is a neighbor of mine who not only plays several instruments and gives lessons but sews as well, I finally went to see for myself what she was making.

There in her sewing room hung a sheer, lace-trimmed nightgown and a yellow, lace-trimmed slip. Folded on a table were several pairs of panties (one pair was yellow to match the slip), while on the sewing machine was a yellow girdle that she was just finishing. She still planned to make a yellow bra to complete the ensemble for her daughter's birthday.

When she told me how little in time and money the lovely garments cost, I decided to try making some lingerie myself. I found out that it is not only quick and economical but easy and fun besides.

The whole thing seems to have started in Minnesota. Women in the Twin Cities have been making their own undies for years. Recently, however, this interest in making your own lingerie has spread to other parts of the country.

Probably the most popular fabric among home seamstresses is the 40 denier nylon tricot, which is used for slips, panties, bras, nightgowns, etc. There is also a 15 denier tricot, a very sheer nylon, that is used for nightgown overlays, peignoirs, armhole and neck bindings, and such "notions" as curler bonnets and scarves. There are stretch materials for girdles, power net (lycra), stretch satin for panels, and stretch lace for trim. There are brushed, printed, and quilted nylons, laces, and elastics.

Working on knit materials is very easy, though it does require a few small adjustments to the sewing machine. But first of all you will need sharp scissors or barber shears. You ought to have a ballpoint needle. The ballpoint spreads the fibers instead of piercing them and prevents skipping stitches. Set your machine stitch toward "long" (10 to 12 stitches per inch).

To get started on my own project of making lingerie, I sent to a manufacturer in Minnesota and ordered 1 lb. nylon tricot. I ordered some laces and elastics, too. The whole order came to $4.64, including the extra $1 for postage and insurance. (They returned my change stuck to my bill of sale with the order.) I made at least a half dozen garments from 1 lb of tricot.

Of course they sell by the yard, too, as do most other fabric houses. One yard of material will make several garments as the tricot is about 108 in. wide.

Girdles and other garments made of power net should be made with a zigzag stitch, but most of the other undies can be made with a straight stitch. If you use a straight stitching machine, two stitchings close together on seams make a more durable garment. This stretches in the same way that the fabric stretches.

You may have to adjust your tensions. If your stitch loops on the top side of your garment, your bobbin tension is too loose. If it loops on the bottom side, your top tension is too loose.

BRIEF

For the brief you will need nylon tricot, ½ in. elastic for the waist, and ¼ in. elastic for the legs. Lingerie elastic can be supplied by the fabric houses in colors to match tricot. It is softer than the elastic with which you are familiar.

I used a Sew Lovely Lingerie pattern because it comes in five sizes. It takes a bit of time to trace off your particular size but, if there are several feminine members in your family, it means quite a saving compared with buying patterns of one size at a time. However, there are different sized patterns put out by other houses.

Tricot is a one-way stretch material, so your pattern is placed so that the stretch will go *across* the garment—or in the direction in which you need the stretch.

When sewing side seams, hold firmly before and behind the machine foot. If a straight stitch is used, sew side seams twice, one beside the other, and then trim close. All lingerie seams are ¼ in. wide. For pinning, silk pins work better than regular straight pins.

Fig. 10-1. Sew the bottom of the panty back between the two crotch pieces.

After side seams are sewn you are ready to proceed to finishing this easy project. Sew the bottom of the panty back between the two crotch pieces (Fig. 10-1). Sew the inside crotch to the bottom of the panty front (Fig. 10-2). Now bring the outside crotch around the panty as shown in Fig. 10-3. Sew it to the already seamed front and crotch and turn (Fig. 10-4).

Cut $\frac{1}{2}$ in. waistband elastic 3 in. shorter than the waistline and stitch together.

Thinking of the stitched place as the back of the elastic, divide it in half to find the front; then divide again. Mark the four places, and then pin the stitched place on the elastic at the back of the panty, wrong sides together and $\frac{1}{4}$ in. down from the raw edge of the waistline. Continue pinning, matching marked places on the elastic with the front and sides of the panty $\frac{1}{4}$ in. from the raw edge and with the picot edge of the elastic down. Stitch on the elastic on the edge farthest from the raw edge of the panty. Trim the panty edge and turn the elastic to the right side of the panty and stitch on the opposite edge of the elastic.

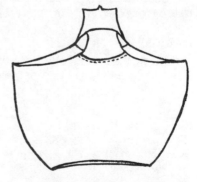

Fig. 10-2. Sew the inside crotch to the bottom of the panty front.

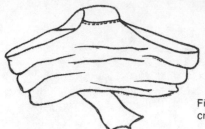

Fig. 10-3. Bring the outside crotch around the panty.

For the panty legs use ¼ in. elastic and cut it 2 in. shorter than the actual measurement. Pin the elastic to the panty leg without stretching it in the crotch area. Sew according to the previous directions. You can use either zigzag or straight stitching.

SLIP

Three yards of lace will trim a slip, see Fig. 10-5. When trimming the slip bodice, lay the edges of the lace and bodice together, the lace over the bodice, and pin them together. The corners of the lace will be mitered (Fig. 10-6) at points where the straps attach. To miter, see Chapter 18. Topstitch the mitered corner but do not stitch it to the fabric of the slip. Hold the lace and fabric firmly when sewing but do not stretch. It is best not to cut the lace until it is sewn to the material. Sew the lace to each bodice section before joining the sections. After the bodice is joined together, you can either trim away the slip material beneath the lace or you can stitch the lace to the slip at the top of the garment. Raw edges will not ravel.

The lace at the bottom is applied in the same way as the lace at the top. Or the slip may be hemmed narrowly by machine or hand.

Shoulder straps can be bought ready-made or they can be made from the tricot or from satin ribbon.

HALF-SLIP

No pattern is needed for the half-slip shown in Fig. 10-7. Use an old half-slip for a pattern or make a paper pattern this

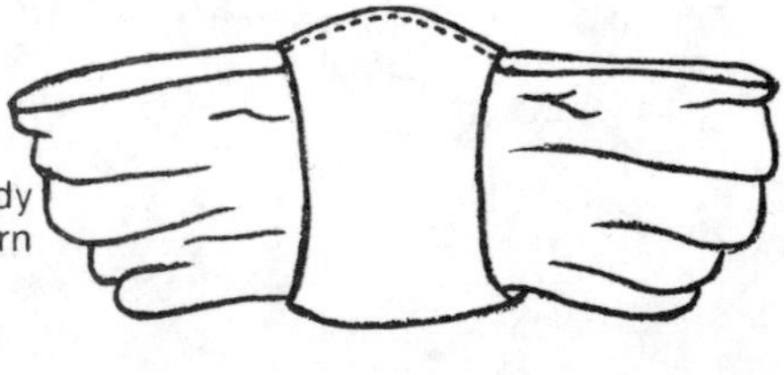

Fig. 10-4. Sew it to the already seamed front and crotch. Turn the panties right side out.

Fig. 10-5. Slip.

way: Cut a rectangle of paper 11 in. wide and as long as needed. (This pattern will be one-half of either the front or back; in other words, place it on the fold of the material and cut the two alike.) Pin the side seams and stitch, keeping your hands before and behind the needle to hold the material firm. Stitch the seams again; trim close. Finish the bottom with a

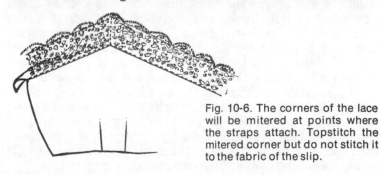

Fig. 10-6. The corners of the lace will be mitered at points where the straps attach. Topstitch the mitered corner but do not stitch it to the fabric of the slip.

Fig. 10-7. Half-slip.

hem or lace. Finish the waist with ½ in. elastic as in the panty directions. This half-slip will fit a size 10.

NIGHTGOWN

Cut the gown (which will be called "lining") from nylon tricot according to your pattern. Cut the overlay from nylon sheer. Sew the side seams of the lining and overlay them separately. Place the overlay on the lining and sew the shoulder seams together. Baste the overlay to the lining by hand or with a long stitch on the machine at the armholes and neck. Narrowly hem the lining by machine or by hand. Hem the overlay or edge with lace as for the slip, see Figure 10-8.

To finish the neck and armholes, cut a strip of nylon sheer across the material (with the stretch) 1½ in. wide and as long as needed as shown in Fig. 10-9. Fold lengthwise and sew the raw edge of the strip to the raw edge of the neck or armhole on the right side using the narrow seam. Trim and turn to the wrong side of the gown. Stitch down by hand (Fig. 10-10).

92

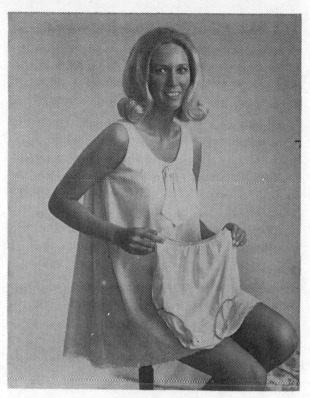

Fig. 10-8. Nightgown.

(Hint for finding right and wrong sides of nylon tricots: Stretch the material crosswise, and it will always curl to the right side.)

JUNIOR BRA

You can use an old bra as a pattern. Cut the cups across the tricot (with the stretch). Cut the side pieces lengthwise.

Fig. 10-9. To finish the neck and armholes, cut a strip of nylon sheer across the material (with the stretch) 1½ in. wide and as long as needed. Fold lengthwise and sew the raw edge of the strip to the raw edge of the neck or armhole on the right side using the narrow seam.

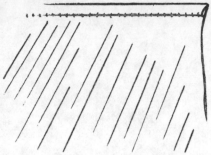

Fig. 10-10. Trim and turn to the wrong side of the gown. Stitch down by hand.

Cut two each of the side pieces and both cups. For the stretch area between the cups use a scrap of Lycra (Power Net). Sew the lining and bra together separately. Join the two, remembering to insert the straps at the front and back. (When finished, you will have a bra of double thickness as shown in Fig. 10-11.) For closure buy a "bra back repair" at your fabric store and attach it.

PADDED BRA

Bra filler is available at knit fabric houses. Sew bias tape over any inside seams to avoid irritation to the body. Finish with "bra back repair" (Fig. 10-12).

GIRDLE

If you have learned to expect to pay $10 or more for your girdles, you will be delighted with the economy and ease of making your own. You may want to make more than one—which you can do easily in an evening. The stretch materials come in colors to match other undergarments. There are power nets for lightweight girdles and garter belts and Jacquard Lycras for garments of more strength. For body

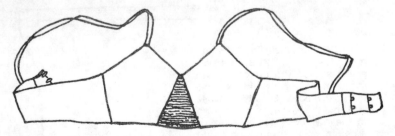

Fig. 10-11. Join the two (lining and bra), remembering to insert the straps at the front and back.

Fig. 10-12. Padded bra.

comfort use a plush elastic for the waist and legs and apply it the same way as elastic to the panties. (Plush elastic comes in colors to match the Lycra.)

If you plan a panty girdle, the leg of it should not be more than an inch smaller than your leg measurement. If your girdle will be made of heavyweight stretch fabric, you may want to make it with a pattern a size larger than your panties.

Ideally you would use a zigzag stitch to sew a girdle; however, it can be done with a straight stitch if you stretch the material as you sew and then sew each seam two or three times.

TURTLENECK SHIRT

The material you will be using for this garment will be a cotton knit. Stretch the material as you sew. It will spring back into place (Fig. 10-13).

Using ¼ in. seams, sew the shoulders. Cut a strip of necking according to a pattern or about 17 in. long. (Necking can be bought to match the color of the shirt fabric.) Sew the

Fig. 10-13. Turtleneck shirt.

end of the necking together to form a circle, and then sew the folded circle to the neck edge, stretching as you sew. Stitch again. Lay the shirt out flat and sew in the sleeves. Stitch again. Sew the side seams from the edge of the sleeve to the bottom of the shirt. To finish the sleeve measure off a strip of necking material the length of the sleeve edge and 2¼ in. wide.

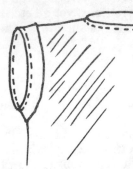

Fig. 10-14. Sew the strip to the armhole with the right side of the strip to the wrong side of the shirt.

96

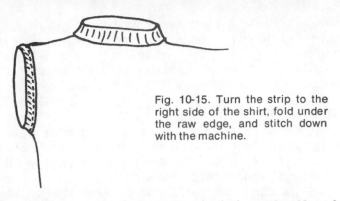

Fig. 10-15. Turn the strip to the right side of the shirt, fold under the raw edge, and stitch down with the machine.

Fold crosswise and stitch the end of the strip. Now fold lengthwise and sew the folded strip to the edge of the sleeve, right sides together. Turn down to form the cuff. Hem the bottom of the shirt.

For a sleeveless shirt, cut the armholes 1 in. higher and bind them with a diagonal strip of fabric 1¾ in. wide and as

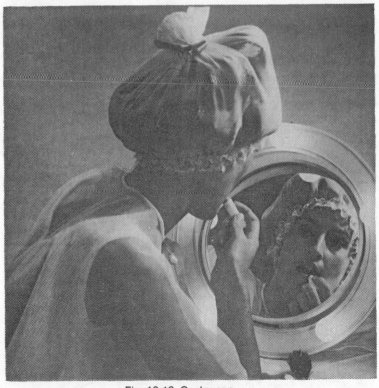

Fig. 10-16. Curler cap.

long as the armhole. Seam the armhole strip. Seam the sides of the shirt. Sew the strip to the armhole with the right side of the strip to the wrong side of the shirt as shown in Fig. 10-14. Turn the strip to the right side of the shirt (Fig. 10-15), fold under the raw edge, and then stitch down with the machine.

CURLER CAP

Cut (crosswise of fabric) two rectangles of nylon sheer 18 in. wide by 12 in. long. Seam the short sides together. Cut ¼ in. elastic 1 in. shorter than the head measurement and apply it to one of the open ends according to directions for the panty. (If you like, you can apply the lace at the same time as when stitching the elastic to the right side of the material.) Gather the opposite end of the cap by running a long stitch around it by hand or machine about 2½ in. down from the opening. Pull the thread to gather it as tightly as possible. Stitch back and forth to hold the gathers. Tie a ribbon over the stitching (Fig. 10-16).

MAKEUP CAPE

Cut a pattern from paper for one-fourth of a circle so that it will have a radius of 17 in. (the completed circle will have a diameter of 34 in.; see Fig. 10-17).

Fold a piece of nylon sheer both lengthwise and crosswise, and lay the pattern on the material so that both radii of the quarter circle fall on the folded right angle of material (Fig. 10-18). Cut out the circle. Mark with a pencil the center of the circle, and then open out the material. Place a cup upside down over the mark and trace around it. Cut out the hole for a neck opening. Fold the circle in half and slit it up to the neck for a front opening. Deepen the neckline in front by 1 in. (or as

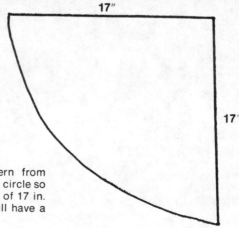

Fig. 10-17. Cut a pattern from paper for one-fourth of a circle so that it will have a radius of 17 in. (the completed circle will have a diameter of 34 in.).

98

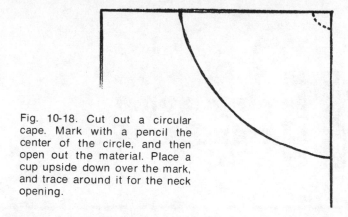

Fig. 10-18. Cut out a circular cape. Mark with a pencil the center of the circle, and then open out the material. Place a cup upside down over the mark, and trace around it for the neck opening.

needed for a comfortable fit). Bind the neckline with nylon sheer strip as for the nightgown neckline. Hem around all the edges with a machine or by hand. Sew a small snap at the neck opening. Add ribbons if desired.

Once you start sewing on stretch fabrics you will think of many more things to make: bra-slips, cardigans, pajamas, mules, tote bags, curler bags, scarves, etc.

 # Handsome Handbags

To make one of the beautiful handbags shown in Fig. 11-1 you will need upholstery or drapery samples. Try the furniture, drapery, and department stores. You can probably buy last year's samples for 35 cents to $1. After that, if you don't have suitable material on hand, you will need to buy only lining material, something for bag handles and, perhaps, interlining. These make such elegant gifts for so little that you can give them all year long for birthdays, graduations, Christmas, personal showers, and for no reason at all. Or you might want to sell them at a bazaar or at one of the popular boutiques that feature handmade items.

Whether the bag will be a zipper bag, one with a flap, or an evening bag, the size will be determined by the number of small swatches attached to the large sample, for these small swatches will be sewn together to become colorful patchwork fronts for the bags. Some of the samples will have two or three rows of the small swatches showing various colors of the same fabric as in Fig. 11-2. Ordinarily these will make the largest bags.

Sometimes, however, you may want to cut off enough of the large sample to get rid of the needle holes that may be left by the stitching when the small swatches are removed (especially on velvets). Sometimes I do not cut the sample, but instead I cover the needle holes (on the backs of the bags) by machine stitching over them a matching bias tape, good quality ribbon or braid, or even lace. Some fabrics will not show the stitching holes.

ZIPPER BAG

When there is not enough material to fold over for a flap, I make a bag to be closed with a zipper, as shown in Fig. 11-3.

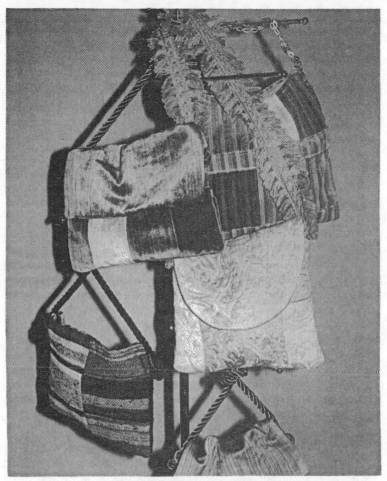
Fig. 11-1. Handbags from scraps.

(There is another way of closing such a bag with a self-adhering tape that goes under the trade name of Velcro, which I shall mention later.) In any case, the first thing to do is to cut straight across the top of the large sample to get rid of the two large grommets there. The large sample will be the back of the bag. Next you will make your bag front. You may have to trim off a bit of each small swatch to make them of a uniform size to fit the size of the large sample. Arrange the colored swatches to please the eye, and sew them together. Trim the back and front to fit if necessary.

Sew the zipper in *before* sewing the back and front together like this: Turn down the top of the front of the bag ¾ in. to the inside. About ½ in. down from the folded edge, lay

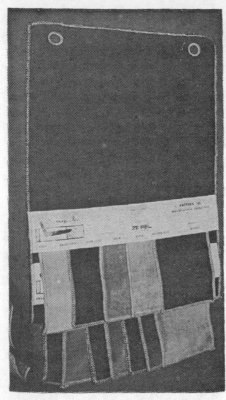

Fig. 11-2. Large sample with small swatches (in various colors) of same fabric.

one side of the zipper, right side up, along the folded hemline so that the cloth ends of the zipper will be even with the sides of the bag (the full length of the zipper should measure the same as the width of the bag). Topstitch the zipper to the folded edge with a very small seam. On the back of the bag, fold to the inside ¾ in. of the top edge and stitch the other edge of the zipper along the fold ½ in. down from the fold line with the zipper face up. Now, with the right sides of the bag together, stitch the side seams, catching in the cloth ends of the zipper. Stitch again for a firm hold. Stitch the bottom of the bag then stitch again. Make ½ in. seams.

Lining

While the bag is still wrong side out, use it to make a pattern for the lining. Make the width of the pattern at the top of the bag the same as the width of the bag, but taper it to ¼ in. smaller on each side at the bottom. Add ¾ in. to the length of the pattern for turning under the lining at the top. Turn the bag right side out and begin work on the lining.

Fig. 11-3. Zipper bag.

Place the pattern on the lining material and cut out two pieces. With the right sides together, sew the lining backs to the fronts with ⅝ in. seams. Without turning, insert the lining in the bag so that the wrong sides will be together. Turn under the top edge ¾ in. just beneath the zipper and pin it in place; then hand stitch.

If you prefer, here is a way to close your bag without a zipper: Buy about 2 in. of self-adhering tape in a color appropriate for your bag. (In this case, *do* sew bag together at the sides and bottom before applying the closure tape.) Turn the bag right side out. Then turn to the inside about 1 in. of the top edge for a hem. Machine stitch in a matching thread. Attach one part of the tape (it comes in two parts, one side locking to the other when it comes in contact) midway along the hem of the front of the bag. Attach the other part of the tape midway of the hem on the back of the bag. Line according to previous directions.

Shoulder Strap

Because your samples do not provide material for straps, you can use your imagination. For the velvet bag pictured, I

103

happened to have a strip of velvet close enough in color to the bag to make a shoulder strap, but webbing would have done as well.

I cut two strips of the velvet 34 in. long and 2½ in. wide, sewed them together with ¼ in. seams, turned them, and then, because the material was soft, I made six lengthwise rows of topstitching in matching thread for firmness. Turning under both ends of the strap, I machine stitched them over the side seams about 2 in. down from the top of the bag.

BAG WITH FLAP

The back and the flap of this type of bag (see Fig. 11-4) is made from one continuous piece of material (the large sample). The front is made of the small, varicolored swatches again. In general the size of the front will determine the amount of material left over from the back to make the flap. However, it is good to have a fairly generous size flap even if

Fig. 11-4. Bag with a flap.

you must trim the front a bit smaller to give you more material for the flap. This bag will be closed with 1 in. of self-adhering tape, sewn half to the flap lining and half to the patchwork front. Some of my flaps were cut straight across, and some were rounded; but all had to be trimmed to get rid of the grommets in the top of the large sample. As before, seam the front to the back at the sides and bottom with the right sides together.

Lining

For this bag the lining is made in two pieces, one for the envelope part of the bag and one for the flap (see Fig. 11-5). Cut the lining for the envelope the same width at the top as the bag, but taper down the sides to ¼ in. narrower at the bottom. Cut the lining for the flap 1½ in. longer than the bag flap. Cut an interfacing for the flap from some firm material but *without* the additional 1½ in. (Sometimes I made only a partial interfacing.)

Make a pocket (to be sewn in the lining) like this: Cut a piece of material 6 in. wide by 5 in. long. Turn under and press

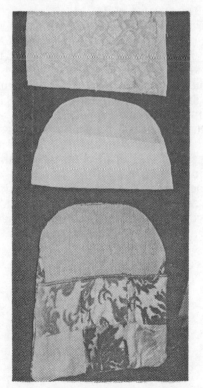

Fig. 11-5. Linings for bags.

½ in. on the bottom and side edges. Crease under ¼ in. at the top of the pocket, then turn down 1 in. more and hem by hand or machine.

Seam the bottom of the envelope lining together, right sides together, but do not seam the sides yet. Instead, open out the envelope right side up. Find the middle of the top edge of the lining back and sew the pocket in place 1½ in. down. Now fold the lining together and sew the side seams.

With the right sides together, seam the front edge of the lining to the front edge of the bag. Turn the lining over and push it to the inside of the bag.

The flap lining should be interfaced to give firmness for attaching self-adhering tape to the lining. Stitch the interfacing to the wrong side of the flap lining with a long (basting) stitch with a ⅜ in. seam around the rounded edge of the flap. Let the opposite edge of the interfacing go free. Now turn the flap over lining side up, fold it to find the middle, and mark it with a pin at the rounded edge. About 1 in. down from this point, sew a 1 in. piece of self-adhering tape (Fig. 11-6). The other half of this piece of tape will go on the front of the bag, so choose a color to go well with the color sample on which the piece of tape will be sewn (Fig. 11-7).

With the right sides together, sew the flap lining to the bag flap and turn it right side out. Turn under the raw edge of the flap lining, press, and pin it in place over the raw edge of the envelope lining and hand stitch.

Close the flap over the front of the bag to find the right place to sew the other half of the self-adhering tape and machine stitch it twice to make a secure closing.

I used a variety of materials for handles on these bags. I used 1 yard of metal chain, doubled (it's cheaper in hardware stores than in fabric stores). I sewed this lightweight chain at the side seams with tough matching thread.

I used 2 yards of fringe in coordinating color, cutting it in half and sewing the top edges together, flat, with a double seam so that the fringe extended out from both sides. Then I turned under the ends and attached them at the side seams.

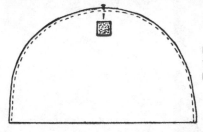

Fig. 11-6. About 1 in. down from this point (middle of flap), sew a piece of self-adhering tape.

106

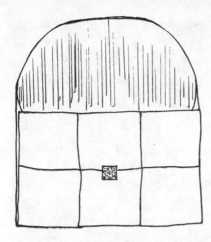

Fig. 11-7. The other half of this piece of tape will go on the front of the bag, so choose a tape color to blend with the bag color.

But the type of handle I used most often was made of a silky cording to match the bag as closely as possible. For each handbag I bought 1¼ yards of cording. The first thing to do is to sew the cut ends of the cording over and over with a needle and thread to keep it from raveling. After sewing the ends, tie a knot about 1 in. above each end. After tying the knot, fold the 1 in. of cording back against the cording handle and hand sew this double thickness of cording at the side seams and 2 in. down from the top of the handbag.

When it is sewn securely in place, you can cover the stitching with a strip of leftover bag fabric. To do this, cut a bit of bag fabric 4½ in. long by 2 in. wide (narrower if you lack material). Fold it lengthwise so that the raw edges meet underneath the strip. Fold under each end of the strip and, then, sew over the place where you hand sewed the cording at the side seams. If your material isn't too heavy, you may be able to machine stitch this strip at either end to cover the cording. Otherwise you will have to secure it with hand sewing.

EVENING BAG (CLUTCH)

There will be some samples that will have only one color swatch attached. That leaves you only the large sample to work with, but this can make a lovely evening bag. I much prefer it to the usual evening bag because there is room for all the things that most evening bags cannot contain.

The bag shown in Fig. 11-8 is made like the bag with the flap except that the whole bag is of one piece—front as well as back and flap. Fold over about 5½ in. for the envelope part of the bag. The rest will be the flap. Round the flap to get rid of the grommets.

Fig. 11-8. Evening bag.

Make the lining in two parts: envelope and flap. Also cut interlining for the two parts to give needed firmness. Put them together as was done for the preceding bag.

Practical and Pretty Doormats

Doormats, personalized with the name of the recipient, are easy to make from carpet samples for weddings, showers, birthdays, and other gift occasions. For Christmas gifts I substitute the word "NOEL" for the name of the person (Fig. 12-1). A green mat with red lettering makes a gay doorway or fireplace mat. One year I made a number of these Christmas doormats and placed them in a small shop where the operator sold handmade items. Some of my Christmas mats were green with red lettering, and some were red with green lettering.

When you know you are going to do this, the trick is to center your "NOEL" lettering on both carpet samples, cut out the letters, and then switch them from one carpet sample to the other. When I had no more red carpet samples, I made a pink and pale green "NOEL" doormat for a friend who has a pale green living room.

If you plan to make a personalized mat for a gift, it is nice if you happen to know the colors of the room into which the doormat will lead. Then you can choose colors to harmonize. The one pictured in Fig. 12-2 was dark blue-green with avocado letters to harmonize with a kitchen featuring those colors.

If you make only one doormat to start, buy one medium-size carpet sample (about 18 × 27 in.) for your doormat and one small carpet sample (14 × 18 in.) in another color for your lettering. If you decide to make two doormats while you're about it, then buy two medium-size carpet samples of harmonizing colors (beige and brown, for example), cut the name or greeting out of the center of each, and switch the letters. Making two is scarcely more work than making one.

Fig. 12-1. Christmas doormat.

Look for samples at carpet dealers, furniture stores, and department stores. They should sell for about 50 cents for small ones and 75 cents for medium ones.

Here is a list of materials you will need for your doormat project: carpet samples, a "utility" knife (with a razor blade-type cutting edge), a cutting board, newspapers, old scissors (for trimming letters to fit into doormat), plastic-coated cloth tape, fabric glue (waterproof), and burlap (a piece about 17 × 26 in. for each mat).

The first thing to do is to make the letters you will need for your name or greeting from the patterns given in Figs. 12-3 through 12-5. Then cut them out of construction or other paper. Most of the "legs" of the alphabet characters are made in 1 in. widths; however, do not hesitate to vary this if it helps to make the letters clearer or more pleasing to the eye (as is shown pictured in the letter "O" in GOFF, for example). Other variations could be in the "cutout" portions of certain letters

Fig. 12-2. Personalized mat.

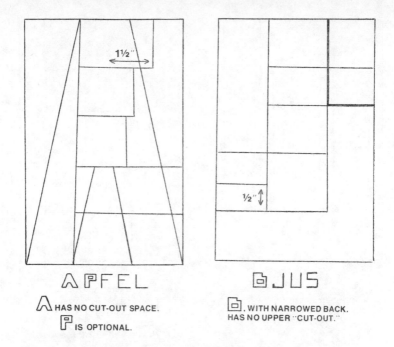

APFEL — A HAS NO CUT-OUT SPACE. P IS OPTIONAL.

BJUS — B, WITH NARROWED BACK. HAS NO UPPER "CUT-OUT."

Fig. 12-3. Left: APFEL, A has no cutout space. Cutout space in P is optional. Right: BJUS, B, with a narrowed back, has no upper cutout space.

that are perfectly recognizable anyway (as in the letter "A" for instance).

After you have cut out the paper letters for your word, place them *backward* and in *reverse* order on the back side of the carpet sample that will provide the letters for your mat. Trace around them. A four-letter name or greeting is ideal, but five or six will work well too. Seven is possible but may look a bit crowded. For this reason, instead of a mat saying "WELCOME," you might think of an alternative such as "HELLO." These greetings are nice for people whose names are too long to work with successfully.

When you have traced around your letters, place the carpet sample on a cutting board or a good thickness of newspapers and cut around the letters with your utility knife or some other sharp instrument.

Now you are almost ready to do the same with your larger carpet sample—but not quite. Before you can draw around those letters, you must center them, because this is the carpet sample that will become your doormat.

Turn your carpet sample to its reverse side and measure off the area that will contain your word like this: Measure in

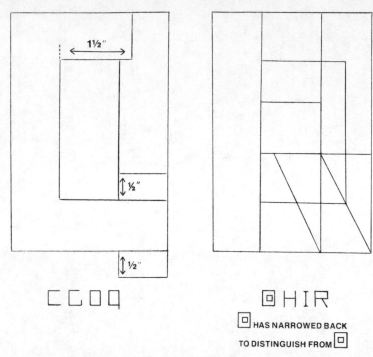

Fig. 12-4. Left: CGOQ. Right: DHIR, D has narrowed back to distinguish it from O.

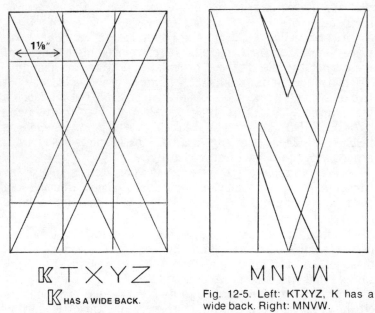

Fig. 12-5. Left: KTXYZ, K has a wide back. Right: MNVW.

from the right side 4½ in. (if your mat will contain only four letters), and make a mark with your pencil. Move your ruler up or down and do the same thing, making a second mark 4½ in. from that side. Do the same at the left side. Now draw lines at each side through those two marks. This will give you the side margins of the area enclosing your letters.

Your top and bottom margins may vary, depending upon how much your carpet sample varies from an 18 in. width. If your larger sample is 18 in., your top margin will be 6½ in. and your bottom margin will be 6½ in. That will leave the necessary 5 in. in the marked-off rectangular area for the height of your letters. In this case you will measure down from the top 6½ in. and make a mark; measure again and make a second mark, and then you will measure up from the bottom 6½ in. in two places and make two marks.

By drawing lines through the marks at the top of the mat and through the marks at the bottom of it, you will have a rectangular area where you will trace your word. *But don't draw the lines yet.* First check to see if your rectangle, when finished, will give you the 5 in. height you will need for your letters. If it will not, then you will have to make those measurements again. If those margins, top and bottom, don't come out to 6½ in. with 5 in. in between them, then give any extra width to the bottom margin. In other words, if the margins won't be the same, top and bottom, let the top one be the narrower one.

After you have marked off your rectangle (Fig. 12-6) by drawing the lines at the top and bottom, you are ready to lay your letter patterns on your mat. Remember to lay them *backward* and in *reverse order* on the back side of the mat. Leave equal spaces between each letter. With four letters the spaces will be about 1¾ in. If your word has more than four letters, the spaces will be narrower. (If you are working with more than four letters, to gain space for the extra letter or letters be sure to make your side margins a bit less than 4½ in.)

After tracing, cut around the letters and lift them out of the carpet sample (Fig. 12-7). Then fill the spaces with the letters you cut from the first carpet sample. You may have to trim those letters with a pair of scissors to make them fit into the doormat. After you have trimmed them to fit, secure them in place with strips of plastic-coated cloth tape. When you have taped all the letters in place vertically to make them more secure, you might want to place two more strips, horizontally, across all the letters, top and bottom.

To give your doormat a finished appearance, cut a piece of burlap to fit on the back of it just inside the binding, squeeze

Fig. 12-6. Mark off your rectangle.

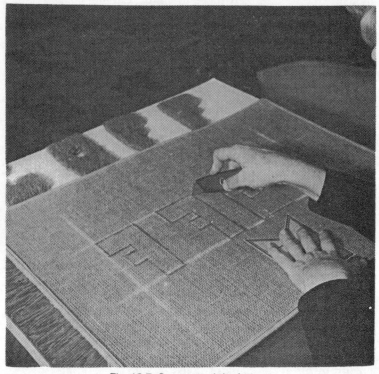
Fig. 12-7. Cut around the letters.

Fig. 12-8. Squeeze waterproof glue on the mat.

Fig. 12-9. Smooth the burlap in place.

waterproof glue on the mat (Fig. 12-8), and smooth the burlap in place (Fig. 12-9).

I can't end without mentioning another hint that many of you may already know: You can carpet a floor with these carpet samples. I did that for my daughter's room using shag samples not only of different colors but of different sizes. The small samples will fit against the larger ones in a hit-or-miss color and size arrangement. Shag is particularly good for a complete floor covering because if the samples contain factory-made holes in one end, the shag will conceal them. (On the other hand, I know of one person who didn't try to conceal the holes. He used clipped samples all of one size, sewed them together, and then tied them with leather thong at the holes for a decorative note.)

A convenient method of putting the samples together is with the plastic-coated cloth tape used for the doormat. A more permanent method is to sew them together with a tough needle and thread on the reverse side. The result in both cases, will be a pretty floor for a small amount of money.

How to Make Shorts

With apologies to those who make only quilts from leftover scraps, here is how to make yourself some shorts that will be the "in" thing. Assemble from your scrap drawer pieces of material that will coordinate well to make a pleasing color pattern. Stick to the same kind of material or at least the same weight. The model on the left in Fig. 13-1 is wearing shorts of all cotton pieces. The one on the right is wearing shorts of corduroy with cuffs of leather (for an elegant touch).

Use a pattern of your own choice, preferably a simple one, but *make* your own material as described below.

Cut squares of old sheeting approximately 12 × 12 in. (I cut my pieces 12 × 14 in. because just one rectangle nicely accommodated the pattern I had chosen to make one front or one back of the shorts.) Lay one of your pretty scraps on the square (or rectangle) of sheeting over at the right-hand edge (Fig. 13-2). Using a long machine stitch, baste this first scrap in place along the edge of the sheeting. Now select another scrap, crease or press down one edge of it, and topstitch the creased edge over one of the raw edges of the first scrap. Select another scrap, crease an edge, and topstitch this edge over another raw edge. Keep applying scraps, creased edges over raw edges, until you have completed a piece of patchwork "material."

When you have completed enough material (I needed only four rectangles, two for the front and two for the back), lay the pieces out on a flat surface and try them in different combinations to find the ones that look best together for the front and back of your shorts. Lay your pattern on the material and cut out your shorts. I used no waistbands or hems. I faced the legs of the cotton shorts with 1 in. bias tape, and I finished the waists of both shorts this way.

Fig. 13-1. Making shorts from scraps. (© 1975 Simplicity Pattern Company.)

In place of a waistband, cut a piece of wide (1½ in.) ribbon or bias tape 2 in. longer than the shorts waistline. With this

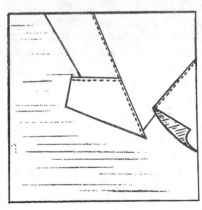

Fig. 13-2. Each new creased edge should cover the raw edges of the previous "patches."

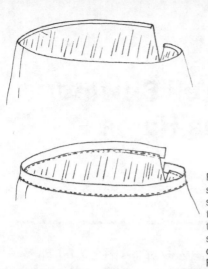

Fig. 13-3. Top: Press down a ⅝ in seam allowance at the top of the shorts. Center: Leaving 1 in. of the ribbon free at both ends of the waistline, apply the wrong side of the ribbon to the right side of the waistline edge. Bottom: Fold the ribbon lengthwise so that the raw edge of the shorts waistline is completely covered.

make a binding to cover the raw edge at the top of the shorts, and then turn it to the inside for a facing for the waistband as follows.

Press down a ⅝ in. seam allowance at the top of the shorts (Fig. 13-3, top). Leaving 1 in. of ribbon free at both ends of the waistline, apply the wrong side of the ribbon to the right side of the waistline edge about ½ in. down from the edge (not quite to the pressed down seam allowance) so that you will make a ribbon extension at the top of your shorts (Fig. 13-3, center). Topstitch. Fold the ribbon lengthwise so that the raw edge of the shorts top is completely covered (Fig. 13-3, bottom).

By topstitching again you will have bound the raw edge of your waistband (catching in the 1 in. extensions at either end of your waistband). Turn your facing to the inside of the shorts, and tack it in place here and there around the waistline.

 # "Scrap" Sewing For the Home

Generally speaking, when the topic of sewing for the home is brought up a person thinks of draperies, slipcovers, and other projects involving large quantities of fabric. However, there are lots of items that can be sewn for the home that could conceivably be made from remnants because they call for only small amounts of fabric. In this chapter we'll take a look at scrap sewing projects for the home, but for good measure we'll throw in a few other items that can't be made from remnants, such as shower curtains and felt tablecloths.

Suppose we go through the house room by room and show what can be made for each one. In the kitchen, for instance, there are lots of handy items you can sew from small pieces of fabric.

The fabric used to make them does not necessarily have to be of a type made expressly for that purpose. If you're planning to sew a toaster cover, for example, your choice of fabric need not be limited to drapery and curtain fabric in kitchen prints. Several times I've taken material leftover from sewing dresses and made bright and attractive toaster covers. And if you have dress fabric that is colorful and washable which would blend with the color scheme in your kitchen, why not use it for this purpose?

My present toaster cover, sewn from a dress fabric, is a red and white flocked gingham check similar to the one shown in Fig. 14-1. Terry cloth, plain or printed, and cottons with floral designs on them make up into pretty and practical toaster covers, too. You can also use two different but harmonizing materials to stitch up a toaster cover.

Here's how to make a toaster cover. Measure the height and width of your toaster front. Add 1 in. to the width to allow

Fig. 14-1. It takes little time and fabric to sew a toaster cover like the one shown here. The arrows indicate how to measure the toaster for a cover.

for the side seams and ½ in. to the length; cut two pieces of fabric to this size. To determine the width of the band that will run between the front and back sections, measure the depth of the toaster from the front to the back and add 1 in. for seam allowances to this figure. (All seams will be ½ in. wide.) Cut the band in this width, making it long enough to cover the sides and the top of the toaster. For good measure make the strip an inch or two longer than is actually required. Then, if the extra length isn't needed, cut away the excess after you attach the band to the front section.

Pin the band to one of the sections, keeping the right sides facing out. Clip the corners of the band to make it lay flat. Stitch; trim the seam. If the band is too long, cut away any extra fabric. Pin the opposite side of the band to the remaining section. Clip the corners of the band. Stitch; trim the seam. Bind the edges with bias tape following the directions given on the package. Slip the cover on the toaster; trim the bottom edges to the proper length and bind with bias tape. Or finish the bottom edges with a fringe trim. A toaster oven cover could be made in the same way.

If you have some fabric left over you might want to trim your window shades in the kitchen to match your toaster cover. All that's needed for each one is a strip of material a little wider than the shade. Here's how it's done.

To determine how much fabric you'll need for each shade, measure the width of the shade and the size of the hem. Add 1 in. to both measurements, and cut a strip of material to this size. Press under ½ in. at the top, bottom, and both sides. Top stitch close to the side edges but not the top and bottom ones. Remove the wood strip from the channel of the shade. Pin the fabric strip over the hem, matching it at both sides with the outer edges of the shade. Topstitch close to the top and bottom edges of the channel and insert the wood strip. If the shade is frayed and you have length to spare, you might want to cut away the worn part and make a new hem in the shade before sewing on the fabric strip.

Pot holders are other items that can be sewn entirely from scrap material (Fig. 14-2). To make the kind that slips over the handle of a pan, cut two pieces of quilted cotton fabric for the front and back sections, shaped as shown, and measuring 3 × 6½ in. at the longest point. Next, cut four wool pieces of the same size and shape for insulation and two from cotton for the lining. Divide the fabric pieces into two sets and layer each with the quilted material on top, the two wool pieces next, and the lining on the bottom. Machine baste the layers together. Bind the top edges of the front and back sections with the wide

Fig. 14-2. Sew a pot holder from layers of wool, cotton, and quilted cotton fabric. The pot holder, bound with wide bias binding, slips over the handle of a pan.

bias binding. Keeping the right sides out, sew the front and back sections together. Finish by binding the pot holder with wide bias tape.

To make a square pot holder, cut leftover terry cloth or quilted cotton fabric into 6½ in. squares. Other firmly woven cottons could be substituted, but you might want to quilt the hot pad if you use them. For the filling you'll need two or three 6½ in. squares of wool, depending on the thickness of both the wool and the outer fabric. Machine baste the layers together. If you're planning to quilt the hot pad, do so before applying the binding. Use the wide bias binding to encase the edges. For best results, round off the corners of the hot pad before binding them.

Remnants can be useful, too, in sewing items for the living room such as a shorty curtain for a transom window, pillows, and armrest covers (sometimes called arm caps) for upholstered furniture.

You can use the smallest of your scraps to sew patchwork covers for your pillows, reserving the medium-size pieces to make pillows in the ordinary way. If you're short of the fabric needed, you might want to combine two fabrics, using one for the front and back sections and the contrasting one for the boxing strip between them. Certain drapery fabrics, slipcover material, and all types of corduroy are good choices for making pillow covers. (See Chapter 6 for more on this.)

Armrest covers can be made from remnants of slipcover or upholstery fabric. The covers will protect your new upholstered furniture or hide the worn areas of older pieces. To make them, cut rectangles 12 × 18 in. in size. Center them on the arms of the chair or couch and pin darts at the right and left front edges to make the covers fit snugly. Stitch the darts as pinned; trim. Press the darts open. Trim both side front edges, rounding them slightly to bring them in line with the sides. Finish all four sides by narrow hemming.

A felt table cover suitable for holiday use (not to be confused with a long tablecloth) can be made for a round coffee table and only requires 1 yard of fabric for a table with a 32 in. diameter. If you can do so, buy the 36 in. width of felt because it is cheaper and you'll have less waste.

To make it, measure the tabletop to find the diameter, then divide this figure in half to find the radius. This is the figure you'll use when drawing your circle. Next, fold the felt in half and put a pencil mark on the fold at a point equidistant from both sides. Open the felt up and spread it out on a table top or other firm, flat surface. If the radius of the coffee table is 16 in., place a yardstick on the center dot and make a pencil mark 16 in. from the center. Moving your yardstick slightly, make another mark 16 in. from the center dot and so on, every 2 in. until the circle is complete. Connect the marks to make a continuous line.

Before cutting into the felt, try it on your table. Center the fabric and place a book on it to keep the felt from shifting. Make sure the pencil marks are at the table's edge. If not, make any adjustments now. Cut out the circle, turn it to the right side, and attach the fringe. A little over 3 yards of fringe are needed to go around a table 32 in. in diameter.

You also can make a floor-length tablecloth, but you will need considerably more felt. Two yards of felt in a 72 in. width will cover a table 32 in. in diameter and 16 in. high. For the floor-length tablecloth you won't be able to use the narrower width unless you compensate by buying more of it and then cut it into sections which you seam together to achieve the extra width.

Make this tablecloth like you did the first one, but change the length of the radius to allow for the longer length. For a table with the above-mentioned measurements, you will need to measure off 32 in. from the center of the fabric. When you try the uncut cloth on the table, check to see if the pencil marks are floor length all the way around. If not, make any necessary changes now. The penciled edges should not drag on the floor but just barely touch it. If the penciled lines do drag, make your circle ¼ in. smaller all the way around. Cut out the circle, turn it to the right side, and attach the fringe. The fringe should be attached in such a way that the outer edges of the tablecloth and fringe are even; otherwise the fringe is liable to trail on the floor. A good vacuuming or airing each week will keep a felt tablecloth fresh and bright looking for a long time.

Sewing a throw cover for your couch is an easy-to-execute project because it calls for only the basic sewing skills. You'll have just two pieces of fabric to join before narrow hemming the throw cover and applying the fringe, and that's all there is to it. True, the pieces of fabric you'll be working with will be large, but the type of material used to make throws is generally not bulky or difficult to work with and you'll have no tucks, darts, ruffles, or fitting to worry about.

Depending on the fabric you select and the price you pay, it should cost you less to sew a throw than to buy one of the better throw covers. Then, too, you might be able to obtain a fabric superior in quality to that in a ready-made cover costing the same amount of money. I sewed my first couch throw from a slipcover fabric in a colorful print and applied a coordinating fringe trim to the edges. The second time around I chose corduroy—it proved to be durable for this purpose.

To make a 70 × 108 in. throw, you'll need 6¼ yards of material; a 70 × 120 in. size would require 6¾ yards. When measuring the length of your couch, remember to allow for the extra fabric which will be tucked in at the back and both ends of the couch. And be sure to choose a fabric with body to it so the throw won't end up in a mass of wrinkles.

Start out by cutting your fabric in half; set one of these pieces aside for the moment unless you're working with material in a 36 in. width, in which case you can skip the next step. Split the remaining piece lengthwise because the combined widths of two 45 or 60 in. pieces would result in more material than is called for. Couch covers generally run about 70 in. wide, so figure on this width when cutting the second piece of fabric. After you've split the fabric and set the leftover strip aside (hopefully, to be used in other projects), seam the two pieces together lengthwise. Round off the corners of the throw and narrow hem the edges. Apply a fringe trim for a decorative touch.

For the bathroom you might want to sew window and shower curtains that match. It's easy to do if you make both curtains from sheets. A twin-size sheet will make the shower curtain with some fabric to spare. Naturally you'll want to use a plastic liner under the shower curtain.

To make the shower curtain, place the sheet on a tabletop or other flat surface. Place the plastic liner on top of the sheet, keeping the left side edges even and positioning the liner so that the top edge is directly over the *bottom* edge of the sheet. Mark the positions of the holes where the hooks will go on the bottom hem of the sheet. Make small-size buttonholes on the hem as marked. Cut away excess fabric along the right edge of the sheet, allowing enough material to turn under for hemming. Hem the right edge of the curtain. Hang the curtain liner and curtain on the shower rod to determine how much fabric to cut away at the bottom of the sheet. Cut off excess material and hem the curtain, making it slightly longer than the liner. A fringe trim would add a nice touch whether it runs across the top (but below the buttonholes), down the side, or near the bottom. But if you trim the shower curtain, you should also do the window curtain to match for a unified look. If you wish you can use the fabric you cut away at the bottom to make a tieback for your shower curtain.

Fabric leftover from making bathroom curtains also can be used to sew a laundry bag that will hold soiled hankies (Fig. 14-3). Here's how you can make one.

Cut two pieces of fabric, 15 × 15 in. Seam them together at the sides and bottom with the wrong sides facing out. Turn it to

Fig. 14-3. Laundry bag, easily sewn from scraps, holds soiled hankies.

the right side. Make a buttonhole at each side seam, starting exactly 1¼ in. from the top edge. Stitch ¼ in. away from the top edge. Turn on the line of stitching. Turn under again to form a 1 in. casing. The top of the buttonhole should now be even with the top edge. Stitch the casing.

To make the drawstrings, cut two 40 in. lengths of bias binding. Fold them in half, matching the outer edges, and stitch. Thread one of the drawstrings through the casing using a safety pin. Start and end at the same buttonhole. Insert the second drawstring in the other buttonhole. Thread the drawstring through the casing, and bring it out through the same opening where it went in. Seam the ends of the drawstrings together, and work them until the seamed parts are hidden in the casing.

Sewing an item for the bedroom such as a spread requires a considerable amount of fabric, but when you're trying to match the design in the wallpaper or drapes, you'd probably do best financially and otherwise to sew your own. There are fabrics available made especially to match wallpaper designs, and a list of these usually can be obtained at paint stores. After checking out the cost, however, I decided to compare prices of similar fabrics at the store where I usually buy material. So, armed with a sample of our bedroom wallpaper, I paid a visit there and managed to find a print that closely resembled our paper and at about $2 less per yard than an exact match would have cost. Because I planned to sew drapes, valances, and the spread from the material, I realized a nice savings by buying the less expensive fabric. If you too are lucky enough to come away with a good match, chances are no one will ever know the difference.

If the material you'd like to use for your spread is quite costly, you can cut the amount needed by not carrying the sides of the spread to the floor. Instead, plan to take it slightly past the top of the box spring and add a dust ruffle which can be pleated, ruffled, or tailored. The dust ruffle can be sewn from a less expensive fabric in a color that matches one found in the design of the spread. If you use an old sheet for the part of the ruffle that fits between the box spring and mattress, you'll save still more money. To make a ruffle by this method, cut the sheet the same size as the box spring, but allow for the hem at the top, the seams at the bottom, and both sides. Then attach the ruffle to the sheet.

The spread itself is not hard to make, but when buying the fabric remember to allow enough extra fabric to tuck in underneath the pillows unless you're sewing separate pillow shams. Also, because the material is not usually wide enough to cover the entire top of the bed (especially a double, queen, or king size one), you'll need to cut two strips of fabric to fill in on both sides. To determine just how wide the strips should be, center the fabric on the bed and measure the distance from the selvages of the fabric to the side edges of the bed. Remember to provide for the seam allowances on both the center front and the side front pieces. The bedspread will look more professional if you insert cording in the side front and side seams.

If you check out the spreads in the department stores, you'll see that many ready-made ones come with this feature. You might want to scallop the side and bottom edges when sewing a spread to be used with a dust ruffle. You can get the scalloped effect by tracing around a plate of the desired size on the fabric.

Dresser covers are easy-to-sew items that can be made with the fabric remaining after you've sewn drapes and spreads for the bedrooms. Or sew dresser scarves from a linen-like fabric or a sheer one. To make the scarves in our bedroom, I cut pieces of material slightly smaller in size than the tops of our dresser, chest of drawers, and cedar chest. I then turned under the raw edges, using a zigzag stitch to do this in order to prevent them from fraying. A coordinating fringe was applied to the edges for a finishing touch. You also can make the longer scarves that hang over the sides of the dresser.

Fig. 14-4. Use strips of leftover print fabric to trim solid color curtains.

In a child's bedroom you could use a linen-like fabric in a white or off-white shade to make dresser covers. Trim them with rickrack in colors to match the walls, bedspread, drapes, etc., and stitch a fringe trim around the edges.

You also can sew dresser scarves from a sheer fabric. Again, you'll want to cut the fabric almost as long and as wide as the furniture tops. Stitch ¼ in. away from the edges. Turn on the line of stitching. Turn under again ⅜ in. and stitch. If you wish, you can add some sort of trim.

When you're sewing curtains from a solid color fabric for the bathroom, bedroom, or kitchen, why not check over your remnants to see if you have a colorful print that could be used as a trim on them? Printed sheets, for instance, not only make attractive curtains in themselves, but they also can be used to trim a solid color curtain (Fig. 14-4).

To make the trim, cut strips of fabric as long as the curtain is wide plus ⅝ in. on each end for turning under the raw edges. Make the strips as wide as you wish, but don't forget to allow ⅝ in. on each side of them. If your remnants aren't long enough, seam several matching pieces together. The seams won't be that obvious anyway because of the print. Press under the raw edges of the strip and stitch them in place after the curtains are completed. That way you can use the hemline stitching as a guide to the placement of the trim. When sewing trim to the curtain, topstitch close to the edges of the trim.

As you can see, sewing for the home doesn't necessarily mean a big expenditure for a large quantity of material or long hours spent measuring and cutting. When sewn up, small quickie items such as those described in this chapter can go a long way toward brightening up a room, and if you're using leftovers, it won't cost you a thing. Moreover, many of the projects can be sewn in one day. Try them and brighten not only your afternoons but also your home.

Cut Children's Clothing Costs

Almost everyone who sews makes clothing for little girls, but how many venture to make boys' clothing? I was hesitant, too, at first, but once I began sewing for my boys I couldn't stop. The reason? Original, snappy-looking clothes at a fraction of their store-bought cost. The overalls outfits I made for my youngest son, however, would be practical for a little girl, too, although you might prefer to give them a more feminine look through the use of appliques, embroidery, or by the fabrics you select.

For just $5, I managed to make a new wardrobe for my then three-year-old son. Today that cost would be higher, but still far cheaper than the price of manufactured counterparts. For that price I sewed six pairs of overalls, three pair in the long version and three in the short version, and two shirts—one in Dacron-cotton and one in checked gingham. Zippers were picked up for 10 cents apiece (these can still be bought quite inexpensively or salvaged from discarded clothing). Buttons came from my husband's castoff shirts.

The same pattern was used to make all the outfits listed above, including the shirts, which came in both a short-and long-sleeved version. Because the shirts required less than a yard of fabric, a store remnant or leftover material from another sewing project could be used to make them.

Use strudy fabrics to sew the overalls (Fig. 15-1). And if the knees do wear out before the rest of the garment, make your own colorful patches from a scrap of fabric in a contrasting color for use on the worn-out part. Or cut the overalls down into short pants to get double the wear out of the garment. For contrast, especially when working with a solid color, topstitch the tabs and sew the buttonholes in a different

Fig. 15-1. Make these overalls in the short or long version for summer or winter wear. (© Simplicity Pattern Company.)

color. Or cut the tabs from the same fabric as the shirt to be worn with the overalls.

You can use up your odds and ends of hemming tape when hemming the overalls. And as long as the fabric isn't sheer (which would be unlikely anyway in this case), you can use almost any color. If you don't have enough tape of one color for both legs, use a different color for each pant leg. You can even seam leftover bits of tape together and use that for hemming the garment.

Sew the short version of the overalls in lightweight seersucker for summer wear as a sunsuit. On cooler days a shirt could be worn under them. For winter use sew the suit in wool, acrylic, knit, or velveteen for holiday occasions. Turtleneck shirts would go well with all these fabrics with the possible exception of the velveteen, which would probably require a dressier shirt.

Another item you can make for a preschool child is a "souper" bib (Fig. 15-2). You'll need two fingertip towels and bias binding in a contrasting color. Cut a half circle opening in each towel at the center top for the neck. Sew the two towels together at the top on the left side only to form the shoulder seam. Bind the entire neck and opening edges. Make two buttonholes at the top of the towel on the open end, and sew two buttons opposite the buttonholes. This bib offers protection even for school-aged children who come home for lunch at midday.

Anyone who sews for a toddler also might like to make the youngster at least one pair of felt suspenders. The suspenders will prevent the child's pants or skirts from dropping down below his or her tummy as they are inclined to do. The suspenders are sewn from two felt squares in contrasting colors for a total cost of under $1. The suspenders can be cut out with either a pinking or scalloping shears. Here's how it's done.

Measure one piece of the felt and divide it into five equal sections, running the length of the felt as shown in Fig. 15-3. Place the second felt piece underneath the first one, keeping the outer edges even. Cut out the felt strips through both thicknesses. To make the crosspieces, cut one of the strips in half, again through both thicknesses. Set aside crosspieces for the moment.

Separate the two thicknesses of felt. Sew two long strips of one color together end to end. Do this with all eight long strips. Press the seams open with your fingertips.

Topstitch two crosspieces of contrasting colors together, keeping the outer edges of both layers even. Do the same with the remaining two crosspieces. To determine placement of the crosspieces, try one suspender on the child (wrong side up), and pin the crosspieces in the correct position on the wrong side of the suspender. If the straps are too long, cut them down to size.

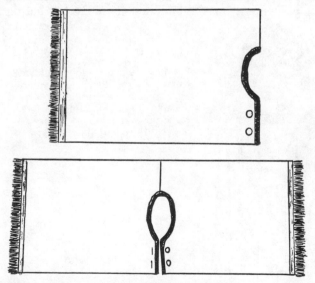

Fig. 15-2. Sewn from two fingertip towels, the "souper" bib shown here will protect the clothes of a young child.

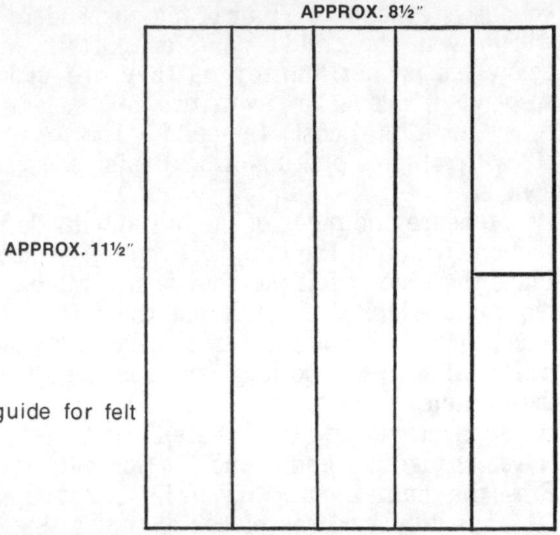

APPROX. 8½"

APPROX. 11½"

Fig. 15-3. Cutting guide for felt suspenders.

Take the long strips of one color and place them on the top of the strips of a contrasting color, wrong sides together, with the ends of the crosspieces sandwiched between the two layers. Keep the outer edges even, and top stitch fairly close to the edges, catching the ends of the crosspieces as you do this.

Try the suspenders on the youngster to determine the correct placement for the buttonholes. Make the buttonholes

Fig. 15-4. Felt suspenders such as these can be easily and inexpensively made from two felt squares in contrasting colors. Make several pairs in colors to match different pants or skirts.

132

as marked. Sew buttons on the inside waistbands of the pants or skirts that the child will be wearing the suspenders with. You can decorate the suspenders with appliques cut from felt scraps, such as the red and white sailboat which adorns the white and pastel blue suspenders shown in Fig. 15-4.

Vests are an item that you can sew for children ranging in age from toddlers to teenagers. Store-bought remnants and fabric leftover from other sewing projects are ideal for making them because the yardage called for is usually minimal. Moreover, you can use almost any type of fabric, provided it has body to it. In sewing anything for youngsters, however, you'll probably want to use a washable material such as knit, denim, cotton, corduroy, or acrylic. The vests shown in the illustration were made for boys, but you can sew vests for girls as well.

If you don't have enough of one kind of fabric to make the entire vest, you can sew the front from one fabric and the back from another. Or, for a different effect, you can cut the pockets from a contrasting material. The vest shown at the left in Fig. 15-5, for instance, is sewn from a brown knit and features vinyl pockets in a darker shade of brown. The lining is sewn from a gold Dacron-cotton blend. The vest at the right was cut on the crosswise rather than the lengthwise grain as the pattern instructions called for. This enabled me to take advantage of what material I had on hand leftover from a pantsuit I'd sewn for myself. The end result was quite attractive.

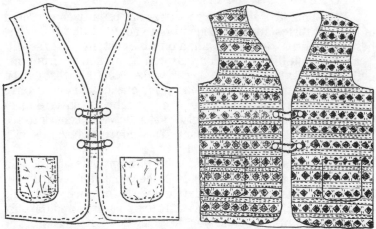

Fig. 15-5. The vest at the left is made up in a solid color remnant with vinyl pockets. The vest at the right is sewn from an Indian print acrylic fabric leftover from making a pantsuit. Actually, the design was intended to be used vertically but, in this case, it was used horizontally with attractive results. (⊂ Simplicity Pattern Company.)

133

Light blue denim with navy topstitching and lining also made up into an attractive boy's vest, as did a pony skin-patterned corduroy with a red lining. A khaki-colored cotton decorated with army vehicles that I found on the remnant pile made up into a novel vest for my youngest son. The light blue denim and the brown knit that I used to sew the other vests also came from the remnant counter, while the corduroy print was a leftover from making a Halloween costume.

Buttons with chain loops attached make attractive closures for vests unless, of course, the front is designed to lap over and button—in which case you couldn't use the chain fasteners. Salvage the buttons to use again, when the vest is outgrown.

Tank tops like the one shown in Fig. 15-6 are another item requiring little fabric. And if you make the tri-colored child's tank top shown here, you can put your leftover knits to work. Ready-made tank tops in this style are available, and doubtless the manufacturer used up his remnants to make them, so there's no reason why you can't do the same. First, though, you'll have to cut apart your pattern into three approximately equal sections. Then, when you cut out the pattern pieces, allow ⅝ in. along each cut edge for the seam. Don't make the first cut too close to the armhole, though. Join the sections together before sewing up the side seams.

HALLOWEEN COSTUMES

Store-bought Halloween costumes are usually constructed of flimsy fabrics and consequently are not very durable. Your best bet, therefore, if you want a durable costume, is to sew it. That way you'll have outfits that can be passed on from one child to the next in line. Or you can make a costume that can be worn for pajamas after the season for ghosts and goblins has ended. Terry cloth and flannel are two fabrics that are ideal for this dual purpose. For safety's sake, however, check to see if the fabric is flame retardant. This information is usually plainly marked right on the bolt.

If time is short you might want to improvise and build a costume around clothing already in the youngster's wardrobe, adding one or two easy-to-make items. For instance, using this method you can come up with a pirate's costume, and the only thing you might have to sew is the vest. You'll need a white or pastel dress shirt, a pair of old pants, and two scarves—one for a head covering and one to go around the waist.

You can make a simple vest by drawing your own pattern on tissue paper, allowing ⅝ in. for the side seams. An

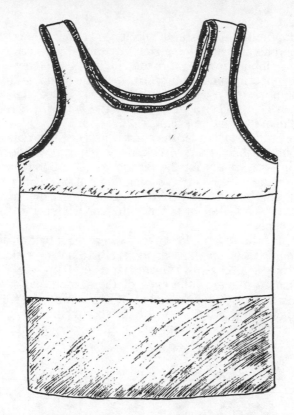

Fig. 15-6. Put your leftover knits to work in this tri-colored tank top.

inexpensive cotton will do for the fabric. You can bind the armhole, neck, and front and bottom edges and thus eliminate the need for a lining or facings. Or you can sew the vest from a pattern.

Cut the pants down to knee length, but don't cut them straight across. Instead, do the cutting in a zigzag fashion so that the edges form points. A rubber dagger could be tucked in the waistband of the pants. Add an appropriate mask and a gold earring, and your child will have a novel and inexpensive costume.

You also can use clothes already in your youngster's wardrobe to improvise a Latin American costume (Fig. 15-7). The only costume part you'll have to sew is the serape, which is trimmed with odds and ends of fringe, braid, and rickrack. If you have these on hand along with a suitable remnant, the serape will cost you absolutely nothing to make, unless you include the price of the thread.

To duplicate this costume you'll need a long-sleeved white shirt (the one shown came already trimmed with red braid), grosgrain ribbon in a ⅝ in. width for the tie, black or dark colored trousers, and a sombrero. If you are unable to round up a sombrero, you can substitute a black flat-topped Halloween derby. Trim the brim of the hat with a red ball fringe to give it a festive look.

The serape, worn over the shirt, was sewn in a red bonded fabric, but any brightly colored sturdy material will do. If you want to use a remnant for the serape, as I did, but do not have a long enough one, join two smaller but matching pieces together, end to end. In a child's size 6, the serape measures 9×50 in. For an older or taller child, you will need to make a longer serape.

To make the serape, first narrow hem the fabric on all four sides. Then gather up an assortment of ball fringe, rickrack in different sizes, grosgrain ribbon, flat braid trim, etc. Pin the ball fringe in place at the ends of the serape and stitch as pinned. A row of rickrack is next in line, sewn 1 in. from the upper edge of the fringe. Sew the grosgrain ribbon 1 in. away from the rickrack. When attaching the rickrack, stitch

Fig. 15-7. With the exception of the serape, all the parts of this costume were taken from the youngster's everyday wardrobe. Red braid trims the shirt, and black grosgrain ribbon was used for the bow. Black pants and a sombrero (an attic find) complete the outfit.

corresponding rows in place at opposite ends of the serape before going on to the next row of trim. Trims should match at both ends in their placement and the type of trim used.

A row of ball fringe is placed 1½ in. away from the ribbon; close to this, sew a row of baby rickrack. Jumbo rickrack, a ⅝ in. width of grosgrain ribbon with gold rickrack sewn down the middle, and another row of jumbo rickrack are all placed ¾ in. apart. If you don't have the particular type of trim that is called for, substitute whatever colorful trims you have on hand.

For best results, measure as you go along so that the rows of trim are even. When working with baby rickrack, hold it in place with cellophane tape while you sew. Peel tape away after stitching.

A variety of costumes can be sewn from a pattern for a zip-front jumpsuit because such a pattern is usually designed with slight variations that allow you to make it up in several versions. If you can possibly do so, buy fabric for costume-making at the end of one season to use the following year. By doing just this I was able to sew a costume and a vest from a pony skin print and even had some fabric leftover. And the material only cost $3!

Zip-front jumpsuits also lend themselves to other costumes. By sewing up the jumpsuit in a solid color and adding patches of contrasting ones, you'll have a hobo outfit. Sew the jumpsuit in a shimmery silver to make an astronaut's suit. For a novel effect, spray paint an old pair of shoes silver to go with the costume. Recently I made a Charlie Chaplin costume for my son using a jumpsuit pattern, see Fig. 15-8. If you'd like to make one, you'll need, in addition to the amount of fabric called for in the pattern, white fabric (an old shirt or blouse will do) and 1 yard of 45 in. fabric in navy blue or black.

To make this costume you'll have to make a few minor changes in the pattern, so plan for this before cutting out the jumpsuit. Because of the tuxedo front, you'll have to insert the zipper in the back seam rather than the front. This won't make any difference in the cutting of the front and back jumpsuit sections, but it will make a change in the facings. Add ⅝ in. to the back facing section along the unnotched straight edge (Fig. 15-9). Then, instead of placing the back facing along the fold line and cutting it in one piece, cut it in two pieces. Cut the front facing in one piece rather than in two as the pattern directs. Do this by trimming or turning under the ⅝ in. seam allowance on the unnotched edge and placing the cut or folded edge along the fold of the fabric. After all the pattern pieces are cut out, sew up the center front seam of the jumpsuit.

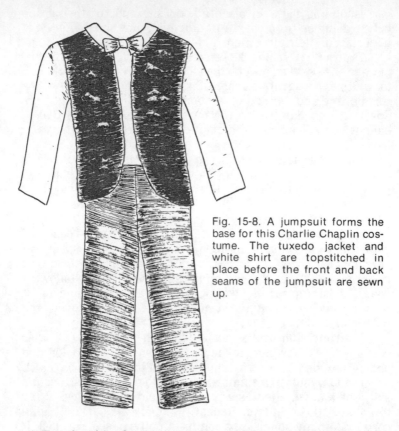

Fig. 15-8. A jumpsuit forms the base for this Charlie Chaplin costume. The tuxedo jacket and white shirt are topstitched in place before the front and back seams of the jumpsuit are sewn up.

For the shirt front, cut a piece of white material 7 in. wide and long enough to extend below the waist of the jumpsuit. Curve the top edge of the white fabric to conform to the neckline curve on the jumpsuit. To make the collar, you'll probably have to use another pattern or make a pattern of your own because most jumpsuit patterns don't include collars. The collar need not extend to the back of the garment: it can be a half collar ending at the shoulder seam. Cut out a collar and an undercollar section. Pin the right sides of the collar sections together, leaving the neck edges open. Stitch as pinned. Trim the seam and points; clip the curves. Turn the collar right side out and press. Baste the raw edges of the collar together. Set it aside for the moment.

Machine baste the white fabric in place at the neckline edge and down both sides. There's no need to turn the raw edges under at the sides because they'll be hidden by the tuxedo jacket. Turn the raw edges of the fabric under at the waistline and topstitch across the bottom edge.

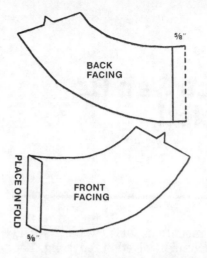

Fig. 15-9. The illustration shows how to alter the facings to correspond with a change in the placement of the zipper.

To make the tuxedo jacket, use the jumpsuit pattern as a cutting guide for the neckline, shoulders, armholes, side seams, and center back. Curve the opening edges of the front sections. Form tails at the bottom of the back sections. Turn under the raw edges of the curved front section and press. Turn under the raw edges of the tails and press. Topstitch the tails. (They will hang free when the garment is completed.)

Pin the front sections of the jacket to the jumpsuit, covering all but the center. Machine baste at the neckline, shoulder, side seams, and armholes. Stitch the curved opening edges of the jacket to the jumpsuit. Pin back the sections of the jacket to the back sections of the jumpsuit, matching the neckline edges, center backs, shoulders, side seams, and armholes. Machine baste. Do not stitch the tails to the jumpsuit.

Follow the pattern directions to finish the jumpsuit with the exception of the zipper, which was moved, and the facings. When the front and back sections are joined together, clip the neck edges where the collar is to be attached. Pin the collar in place and machine baste. Do this before you attach the facings. To complete the costume, add a perky bow tie, derby hat, and Charlie Chaplin mask (if one is available).

Children's clothes and costumes are fun and are inexpensive to sew because you can put your imagination to work thinking up novel ways to use your remnants in making them. The wide selection of children's patterns and the high cost of ready-to-wear clothes combine to make this a good time to sew for youngsters. Try it, and watch the cost of clothing your kids go down.

 # Fabrics Can Be Recycled

You don't have to collect mountains of newspapers and aluminum cans in order to become involved in recycling. You can recycle items right in your own home by making useful articles out of discarded garments, sheets, and curtains. Of course it stands to reason that you won't want to go to all the trouble of recycling an item if the fabric in it isn't worth salvaging. Many times, however, a garment is discarded because it doesn't fit or is out of style. Then, too, perfectly good curtains are often taken down and replaced by new ones when a room is wallpapered, painted, or otherwise redecorated. Sheets can be worn through the middle and still have usable fabric along the sides and bottom. Here is where recycling comes into play.

The good parts of a sheet worn thin in the center can be used in a variety of ways. Sometimes you might be able to sew a pillowcase from the usable fabric. Although you won't always be able to cut one large piece of cloth that can be folded in half and sewn up the way purchased pillowcases are made, this shouldn't stop you from cutting the case in two sections and seaming them together at both sides and the bottom. Use a ready-made pillowcase as a guide to size and to sewing them.

You also can make an ironing board cover from the usable parts of an old sheet. Simply use your present cover as a pattern, and allow enough extra fabric to turn under for the casing. Worn sheets can be cut down and made into contour sheets for a carriage mattress.

Sheets also are useful in making a filling for a chair pad. To make the pad, measure the seat of the chair it's intended for and cut two pieces of fabric ½ in. bigger on all sides than the area you want to cover. Cut several thicknesses of sheeting in this same size, and machine baste the layers together. Pin the sheeting to the wrong side of one of the fabric pieces; machine baste. Trim the edges of the sheeting close to the stitching. If ties are desired, use bias tape that has been folded in half and stitched. Pin the ties in their proper position in the seam, on the right side of the fabric. Stitch across the ends of the tape several times in the seam allowance. Then it won't shift when you're sewing the front and back sections together, and the stitching also will serve as a reinforcement so the ties will not pull out easily.

With the right sides together, pin the padded piece to the remaining piece of fabric. At this point the ties will not be visible. Stitch the front and back pieces together, ½ in. away from the outer edges, leaving an opening for turning. Trim the seams and corners; clip the curves if any. Turn the pad right side out, and use slip stitching to close the opening. Trim the pad with a fringe for a finishing touch.

Using muslin for the outside, you also can sew heavy pads for crib or diaper changes from layers of sheeting or other recycled, washable fabric. Sheeting also comes in handy as a base for crazy quilt patchwork.

A faded pillowcase that's in good condition otherwise can be made into a protective cover for a pillow. If you make your own, you won't have to buy the zippered ones. I don't bother putting in a zipper, preferring instead to slip the pillow in the case and to sew the opening closed by machine. If the pillowcase is too long, I turn the extra fabric to the inside before closing the end. When the cover becomes soiled, cut it open at the end where it was sewn shut, being careful not to cut into the pillow, remove it, and replace it with another one. I've found that this works well because the inner covers don't become soiled as readily as the outer ones and, therefore, don't require frequent replacement.

Curtains are just as useful as sheets for recycling purposes. For instance, if you need something to cover the gap between the bottom of a cafe curtain and the top of an air conditioner, you might want to do as I did and cut one from a discarded curtain (Fig. 16-1). To make it, I used an old kitchen curtain of durable Indianhead fabric and hung it on a rod installed on the lower half of the window frame. The material, although yellow, looked as good as new after an overnight soak in a mild bleach solution.

Curtains that you may have tired of can be used in the garage or cut down to hang at basement windows. Or turn curtains with a cheery kitchen print on them into a colorful apron or covers for your blender, toaster, or toaster oven. If you have a pair of long, ruffled, tieback curtains, you might

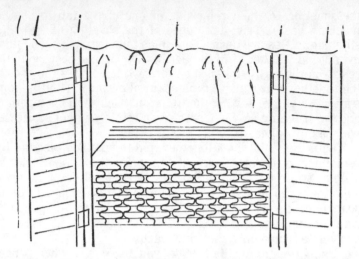

Fig. 16-1. A new curtain was made from an old one to fill the gap between the bottom of the curtains and the top of the air conditioner.

even be able to convert them into a tablecloth, depending on the size of the curtains and of the table you're making it for. To do this you would have to remove the ruffles and heading and straighten any curved edges. Seam the curtains together lengthwise, and hem the edges. A fringe can be added in a coordinating color.

Felt from a table skirt in good condition that for one reason or another you no longer use can be utilized for making a variety of items. A green, red, white, or gold table skirt could be used to sew Christmas tree skirts, Christmas stockings, or other holiday decorations. Felt also can be turned into suspenders, skirts, eyeglass cases, appliques, change purses, and attractive doilies. It comes in handy as a craft material because it doesn't ravel, is available in almost every conceivable color, and is easy to work with.

To make a felt doily like the one shown in Fig. 16-2 to protect your tabletops from scratches and stains, trace around a mixing bowl of the desired size on the felt. Use a colored pencil if ordinary lead won't show up. Cut out the circle and apply a fringe trim. Make the doilies in small, medium, and large sizes to serve different purposes.

A clothespin bag can be cut from a cotton skirt or curtain. Don't let the center back seam of the skirt worry you; simply cut out the back of the bag with the skirt seam in the center. Then line the back of the bag to hide the seam. Let your present clothespin bag serve as a pattern, or make a bag like the one in Chapter 6. Use fabric cut from out-of-style cotton

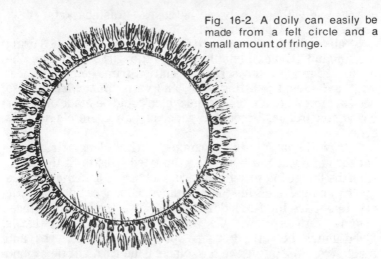

Fig. 16-2. A doily can easily be made from a felt circle and a small amount of fringe.

skirts in bright colors for making patchwork or the six-section beach and jockey hats.

The fringe that's used to trim tablecloths, curtains, and furniture throw covers often outlast the item it's attached to and can usually be salvaged to use in other projects. Fringe can be used to trim new curtains, knife edge pillows, chair pads, doilies, or the serape in Chapter 15. Or glue the trim to

Fig. 16-3. A unique picture can be made from leftover fringe and other sewing trims.

closet and other shelves, hatboxes, wastebaskets, desk accessories, and lampshades.

You also can create a picture like the one in Fig. 16-3 using secondhand fringe. Suitable for a little girl's bedroom, the picture is made from scraps of ruffled trim, hemming lace, felt, lace edging, knitting yarn, and yarn gift tie. You'll also need some sort of a background which could be made of poster board or cardboard-mounted paper or fabric. Here's how it's done.

Draw the lady's figure, complete with a long skirt on the background. Cut the fringe in graduated sizes to fit the skirt. Glue the fringe to the skirt in rows. Cut pieces of hemming lace for the bodice, and glue them in place. Glue lace edging at the neckline. Glue the flat sides of ruffles over the hemming lace, placing them as shown. Sleeves are made from fringe that is glued under the ruffled edges. Cut the head, arms, eyes, and mouth from felt; glue them in place. Glue yarn gift tie around the face to make the hair. Make yarn bows for the pigtails, and glue them in place. If you don't have all the listed scrap items, substitute other trims to create your own original picture.

It's also possible to make a Christmas tree like the one pictured in Fig. 16-4, using ball fringe salvaged from old curtains or tablecloths or leftover from sewing projects. In making mine, I used green as the main color with a sprinkling thrown in of white, turquoise, and red to represent Christmas balls. It took about 225 balls to cover the string cone that I used for the base. If you're buying fringe, figure on approximately 25 balls to a yard of fringe or about 9 yards.

Start by applying glue to a small area at the bottom of the cone and working your way around it, pressing the balls in place. Continue to apply glue to a small area and to cover it with balls until the cone is completely covered. Glue a ball over the hole at the top of the cone. Wind rickrack around the tree to form garlands. Apply glue to the back of the rickrack first to hold it in place. Top the tree with a small angel or star.

Old clothes can be made into new ones, so why not see if those you no longer wear would yield enough usable material to sew a pair of shorts, an apron, or a summer top? If the amount of fabric in the garment is insufficient to provide a garment for an adult, perhaps it could be used to make something for a child.

You can recycle lingerie, too. I had a lovely long negligee which hung in my closet for years although I rarely wore it because the lacy top proved scratchy and irritating to my skin. Then one day I found myself in need of a long slip and hit upon the idea of making one from the negligee.

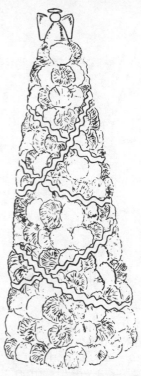

Fig. 16-4. Cut the balls from used and leftover ball fringe and cover a thread or string cone with them to make this decorative tree.

I started out by cutting away the yoke sections and opening up the side seams and hem of the negligee. This left me with three long pieces of nylon fabric, the right and left fronts and the back section. Then, using a short half-slip as a guide to the waist and hip size, I cut the front of the slip from the negligee back. In order to get the true width of the short slip, however, I stretched the elastic in the waistline as far as it would go and added ½ in. to that figure at each side for seam allowances. I also added an extra ½ in. at the top edges because I planned to make a casing for the elastic. In determining the length of the slip as well as the width at the bottom edges, I used a pattern for an ankle-length skirt although I didn't cut the slip quite as full across the bottom as the skirt. The back of the slip was cut in two sections from the right and left fronts of the negligee. An extra ½ in. was added to each section for seam allowances at both the center back and the side.

After seaming the slip sections together, I cut ¼ in. elastic to the size needed plus an additional inch for overlapping the ends. When the ends of the elastic were overlapped and stitched, I placed the elastic ½ in. from the top edge of the slip,

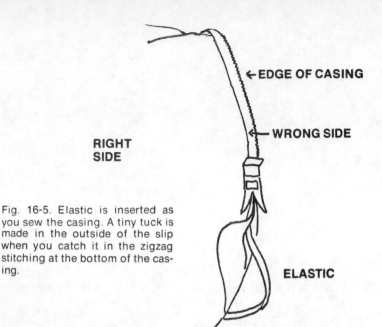

← EDGE OF CASING

← WRONG SIDE

RIGHT
SIDE

Fig. 16-5. Elastic is inserted as
you sew the casing. A tiny tuck is
made in the outside of the slip
when you catch it in the zigzag
stitching at the bottom of the casing.

ELASTIC

on the inside, and folded the top of the slip to the inside over the
elastic. Then I turned the casing to the outside and zigzagged
close to the bottom edges of it, using a small stitch and
catching the outside of the slip in the stitching (Fig. 16-5). At
the same time, I was careful not to twist or stitch through the
elastic. I stretched the elastic when it became necessary to do
so. The bottom of the slip was finished with lace.

To sum up, recycling the available fabrics in your home
can be a challenge to your creativity. And the results of
remodeling clothes and household linens are rewarding
indeed, not to mention the savings you'll realize through your
efforts.

Trimming

FLOOR LENGTH SKIRT WITH APPLIQUE

You can easily make the skirt in Fig. 17-1 without a pattern. Measure off 54 in. for the width of the skirt and 45 in. for the length (or your measurement from waist to floor plus 4 in.). The skirt pictured has only one seam in the back, so the zipper should be placed there. (If you prefer, you can cut two skirt pieces, each about 27 in. wide, and seam the skirt at both sides, placing the zipper in the left side.)

Cut a strip to be folded lengthwise in half for the waistband. Cut it the length of the waist plus 4 in. for seams and lap. Attach the waistband and hem the skirt.

APPLIQUE

To make a Dresden plate pattern on a piece of paper (Fig. 17-2) draw around a 10 in. plate. Cut out the circle you've made, and fold it in half. Fold again to make quarters of a circle. Fold again to make eighths. Measure down 1 in. from the point of the folded circle, and cut out a slightly rounded piece (for the hole in the middle of the finished Dresden plate block).

Now, cutting out one of the eighths of the whole circle, lay it on heavy paper and make your pattern by drawing around the eighth of a circle, ¼ in. out from all edges. Before cutting out your new pattern, fold it in half and extend the length of it by making the bottom round or pointed. Now cut out the pattern. Cut on the *inside* of pencil lines (so pattern won't be too large).

If you do not have enough colors in your scrap box to coordinate with the skirt colors, buy ⅛ yard of different colors.

Fig. 17-1. Floor-length skirt with applique.

Since my skirt material was a kind of silky fabric, I even mixed taffeta and cotton in my blocks for interest.

You will need eight blocks for each Dresden plate. I sewed four Dresden plates around the bottom of the skirt.

Sew the eight blocks together with ¼ in. seams. Press the Dresden plate down flat, then turn under and press down ¼ in. all around the outside edge, clipping where necessary. Clip around the center hole, turn under ¼ in. and press down.

Divide the skirt in fourths to determine where the Dresden plates should be appliqued. Baste them in place all around the outer edges and around the center holes about 3 in. up from the bottom of the skirt. Then sew them very carefully to the skirt by hand so that the stitches do not show.

148

VEST WITH BALL FRINGE

I selected ball fringe in five colors to match the bands of color in the skirt and vest material; however, a number of colors of ball fringe on a plain color vest would be just as attractive.

Buy a plain vest pattern, but stitch it together this way: Sew the underarms. Do *not* sew the shoulder seam yet. Spread the vest out on a table, and arrange strips of fringe across the vest in rows, starting about 2 in. from the bottom. Pin the rows in place about 1½ in. apart all the way to the shoulders. You will need one more short row for the back of the vest than for the fronts. Cut off the strips to proper lengths and topstitch on your machine, using matching thread. (You can pretty well determine before you buy your fringe the amount you will need by spreading out your vest and measuring the lengths of the rows needed for trimming, top to bottom.)

If you don't line your vest, you may sew the shoulder seams at this point and finish by facing all around the garment with bought bias facing material or material cut bias from vest fabric. Snip off any balls in the way of the seams.

To line the vest, do *not* sew the shoulder seams yet. Sew the underarm seams of the vest lining and lay it out against the vest, right sides together. Sew the vest lining to the vest all around the outside. Sew around the armholes and neck, leaving seam allowances for finishing both. Turn it right side out. Machine stitch the vest shoulder seams together, keeping the lining of the shoulder seams out of the way. Now hand stitch the lining shoulder seams together.

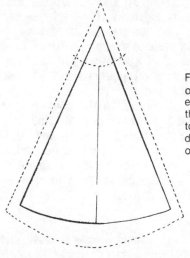

Fig. 17-2. Draw around the eighth of a circle ¼ in. out from all edges. Fold in half, and extend the length of it by making the bottom round or pointed. Measure down 1 in. from the point and cut out a slightly rounded piece.

149

Fig. 17-3. Children's clothes with pockets. (© Simplicity Pattern Company.)

POCKETS

Children love pockets (Fig. 17-3). To add eye appeal and fun to a little girl's jumper or dress, make this triple-decker pocket from your scrap box. The jumper pictured was of avocado corduroy. My scrap box yielded a large pocket of dark green, a medium pocket of blue, and a small one of red. The large pocket was 9 × 7½ in. the medium pocket was 7½ × 6¼ in. and the small pocket was 6 × 5¼ in.

Crease down ½ in. on three sides of all the pockets and press. Crease under ¼ in. at the top of each pocket. Make a 1 in. hem, sewing with matching thread. After hemming each pocket, sew a small pocket to a medium pocket, centering carefully (leaving about 1 in. all around). Sew a medium pocket to a large pocket. Sew a large pocket to a jumper or dress. Then proceed to finish your garment.

Girl's Colored "Patch" Pockets

The jumper pictured in Fig. 17-3 has pockets of different colors, too, but they are made of colored, iron-on patch

150

material. (Buy a packet in different colors.) Cut the pockets any size or shape you like (the ones pictured are lengthwise and crosswise rectangles), that is, one pocket can be long and the other wide. Cut the patch material the exact size you want your finished pockets to be plus 1 in. at the top for turning under. Now cut the pockets from the garment material (this little jumper was denim). Cut this set of pockets ½ in. larger all around than the colored "patch" pockets. Press the "patch" material onto the garment material. Turn under ½ in. on all sides of the pocket. Turn under the hem at the top of the pocket and sew down. Stitch it in place on the dress or jumper.

Boy's "Patch" Pockets

Make "patch" pockets this way, if you prefer. Cut four rectangles of material, each 5 × 6 in. Cover the four rectangles with 5 × 6 in. iron-on patch material in four different colors. On the length of the pocket, make a point if you like. Make a 1 in. hem at the top. Press down ½ in. on the

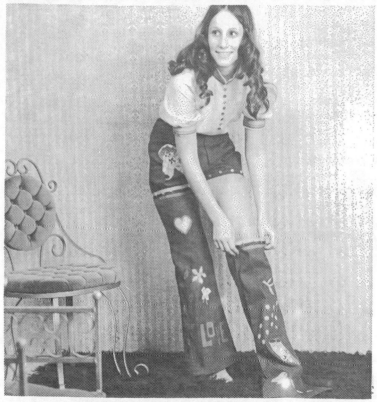

Fig. 17-4. Jeans and shorts combined.

other three sides. Sew the four colored pockets to the pants, two in front and two in back. Sew the pockets on before sewing the side seams of the garment.

MORE JEANS (OR ARE THEY SHORTS?)

Make your jeans completely, being careful not to make them too tight in the thigh area, because further sewing there (when making the shorts) will tighten them a bit (Fig. 17-4).

Cut off jeans to the desired length for shorts, plus ¼ in. (for turning under and facing back a hem). Crease down the ¼ in. and make a hem by facing with 1 in. bias tape in a color to match the jeans.

Crease down ¼ in. on the top of the cut-off legs and turn it down again to make a narrow hem. For the button-on trim extension at the top of each leg, use 1½ in. wide braid (not knitted) or grosgrain ribbon (which may be faced). Cut the ribbon trim 2 in. longer than the measurement around the top of the leg (Fig. 17-5). Seam the ribbon, right sides together, using a ⅝ in. seam to start but tapering to a narrow seam at the opposite side of the ribbon.

Matching the ribbon seam to the crotch seam, lap the *narrow* side of the ribbon to just below the hem you made in the top of the leg and pin in place as in Fig. 17-6. Stretching the leg to fit the ribbon, topstitch it in place. (If the ribbon or braid is lightweight, face it before stitching it to the leg because you will make buttonholes in this extension.)

To face, cut a strip of suitable material 2½ in. wide and as long as your ribbon. Press down ½ in. along each side. Topstitch the top edge of the ribbon to the creased-down facing. Baste the opposite edges. Now make the crotch seam in the faced piece of ribbon, and sew the narrow edge of the faced ribbon to the leg as directed above. The basted facing will be caught in when you do this sewing.

Sew white pearl buttons along the bottom of the shorts every 1½ in. at about the middle of the hemline. On the front of

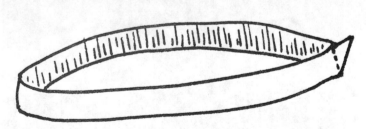

Fig. 17-5. Seam the ribbon using a ⅝ in. seam to start but tapering to a narrow seam at the opposite side.

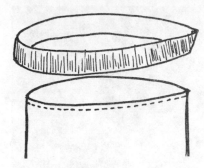

Fig. 17-6. Lap the narrow side of the ribbon to just below the hem you made in the top of the leg.

the legs just before the crotch, instead of a button, sew a black snap (or one to match the color of the jeans). On the back of the legs just before the crotch, substitute black snaps for two buttons. Be sure the part of the snap with the projection sticking out is sewn on the ribbon, *not* on the shorts.

Snap the legs together at the crotch and mark with chalk the places on the ribbon where you will make buttonholes, matching the buttons exactly on the shorts.

To decorate, make your own designs. If you buy iron-on tape in an assorted color pack, you may find some help with patterns and ideas inside the wrapper. You also can cut designs from pretty material and sew them on by hand. Be sure to leave a small edge around the design for turning under. Press the turned-under edge, baste in place on the jeans, and then sew by hand. If you're good at design, make a free hand flower, tree, or bird and embroider it with wool or floss. Let your imagination go wild.

BLOUSE (WITH CROSSOVER FLOSS STITCH)

Decorate a plain white blouse with a short cut cross stitch as pictured in Fig. 17-7 this way: Sew rickrack in different colors and sizes to the front, neckline, or sleeves. To complete the design, embroider it with contrasting floss. Merely stitch over the rickrack with the floss, keeping your stitch on a diagonal. Do not use too long a stitch. For the medium-size rickrack, use six strands of floss; for the baby rickrack, use four strands. You might use green over yellow, red over blue, etc. Teenagers are finding that embroidery is the "in" thing to do, so let your girls try this easy method. It's fun to do the "floss stitch."

DENIM SHOULDER BAG

To make a denim shoulder bag as shown in Fig. 17-7 proceed as follows:

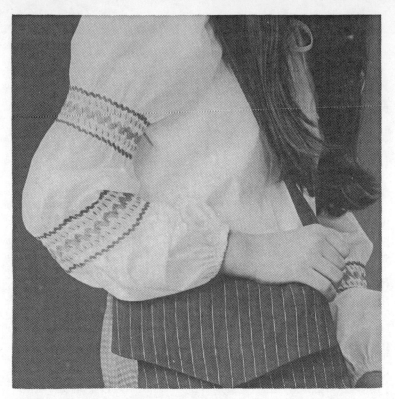

Fig. 17-7. Blouse with trim.

For the envelope of the bag, make a newspaper pattern 11 × 19 in. For the flap of the bag, make a pattern 11 × 9 in. To shape the flap to a point fold it in half lengthwise. Measure down the side 6¾ in. and cut from this place to nothing at the middle of the flap.

Lay the envelope pattern on material and cut it out. Cut out the flap. Cut the interfacing of some firm material for both pieces. Also, cut the lining for the envelope and flap. Cut the flap lining 1 in. longer than the pattern. With a long stitch on the sewing machine, baste the interfacing to the wrong sides of the envelope and flap it close to the edges.

Lay out on the table interfaced bag and flap. With chalk and ruler and starting 1 in. out from the sides, make marks at ½ in. intervals along the top and bottom of both pieces. These marks will be your guidelines for making the white stitching on your bag. (If you prefer to complete your chalk lines top to bottom to make a more visible guide, do so.) Start your stitching at your first chalk mark, 1 in. out from the side of the bag. Sew the rows of stitching at a rather fast, steady speed and your lines will be straighter. Always sew from top to bottom. If you find your material puckering at the bottom of your bag or flap, take out the basting holding the interfacing to the bag fabric.

Right sides together, sew the envelope of the bag together at the sides but leave ½ in. seam allowance at the top. Turn.

Right sides together, sew the lining envelope together at the sides, leaving ½ in. seam allowance at the top. Do *not* turn the lining.

Slip the lining envelope over the bag envelope, right sides together, and seam the front, raw edges together. Turn, pushing the lining down inside the bag. Press the front edge.

Sew the flap lining to the bag flap, leaving a ½ in. seam allowance at the top edge, plus the extra 1 in. Turn and press.

With the right sides together, sew the bag flap to the back, keeping the lining out of the way.

Crease under ½ in. on the raw edge of the lining flap extension and, by hand, sew the extension over the raw edge of the lining inside the bag.

For shoulder straps, cut a strip of material 36 × 3½ in. Crease both sides of the strip. Fold lengthwise, with the creased edges together, and stitch in color to match your bag stitching. Edge stitch the opposite side of the shoulder strap to match. Sew it securely at the sides of the bag about 1 in. down.

MOTHER-DAUGHTER APRONS

To make the mother-daughter aprons as shown in Fig. 17-8, purchase some organdy from the fabric store and proceed as follows:

Organdy comes folded in half. Leave it folded and cut a 16 in. piece off the end for the daughter's apron. (The length can be adjusted by hemming narrowly or deeply.)

Cut another piece 21 in. long for the mother's apron. (Both aprons will be 36 in. wide.)

Cut a strip 6 in. wide off the end of the piece. Cut the piece in half, crosswise. This will make two 18 in. waistbands.

Cut a 3 in. wide strip off the end of the material. Cut this strip in half, crosswise. This will make two 18 in. ties for the daughter's apron.

Cut *two* 4 in. wide strips for ties for the mother's apron.

Cut child's pocket 8 in. long by 7 in. wide.

Cut the mother's pocket 9½ × 8½ in.

Narrowly hem the sides of both aprons. Hem the bottoms to suit the heights of the mother and daughter. Narrowly hem the sashes (Figure 17-8).

Fold the 6 in. wide strip in half lengthwise, and then fold again crosswise. Starting at the sides, cut off 1 in. and taper to

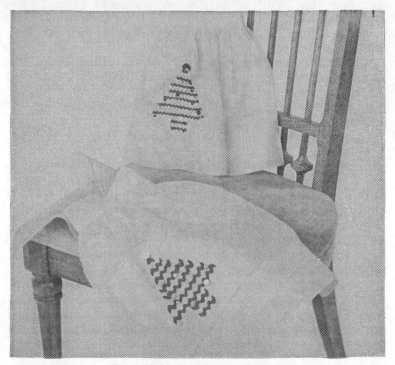
Fig. 17-8. Mother-daughter aprons.

nothing at the middle to round the waistband. Before seaming the ends of the waistband, insert the sash ends, pleated or gathered to fit the width of the waistband end. (The sashes will be inside the waistband when the ends are sewn.)

Gather the apron skirt to fit the waistband. Sew the back edge of the waistband to the wrong side of the skirt. Crease down the front edge of the waistband and topstitch on right side of the apron.

Trims

Make the pockets by creasing ½ in. on three sides. Make a 1¼ in. hem at the top of the child's pocket and a 1½ in. hem on mother's. Do not sew it to apron yet.

Rickrack Christmas Tree on Pocket

Make triangles out of stiff paper 3½ × 4 in. for the child's pocket and 4¼ × 4¼ in. for the mother's pocket. Trace around the patterns onto the pockets, saving room for two rows of rickrack at the bottom for the trunk of the tree.

For the child's pocket, cut seven pieces of green baby rickrack. Cut each piece long enough to fit the triangle design

Fig. 17-9. Christmas tree pocket.

with enough for turning under the raw ends. Space about ¾ in. apart. Cut two short strips for the trunk.

For the mother's pocket, cut green medium rickrack into seven strips to fit the triangle, remembering to cut a bit extra for turning under the ends. Cut the rickrack for the trunk.

Stitch the rickrack to the pockets to form the tree. Stitch the pockets to aprons. Decorate the trees with beads, sequins, tiny toys, and anything else at hand as shown in Fig. 17-9.

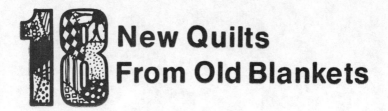

New Quilts From Old Blankets

Figure 18-1 shows five old blankets (actually four old blankets and one old quilt) that, with a bit of magic on the sewing machine, were turned into five "new" quilts. Usually when one thinks of making a quilt, one envisions a project that will take a year or more, but these quilts are for those who need warm covering soon.

MACHINE QUILTED LIGHTWEIGHT QUILT

The first of the three quilts, shown in Fig. 18-2, was the fastest and easiest to make. It was made with only two pieces, the dark plaid blanket pictured and a backing of flannel to make it a warmer covering for a twin bed.

I had bought several yards of good quality flannel when I attended a sale at a fabric house, thinking that I might make some warm sleepwear. When I got home, however, I was faced with the fact that my daughter's two white mice had got out of their cage again and chewed more holes in the double blanket she slept between in the wintertime. So I put my bargain to more urgent use.

To begin my project I had to repair the plaid blanket. To do so I not only cut off the end with the holes but cut away a thin midsection. Then, making use of only the thickest, firmest parts of the blanket, I pieced it back together again with flat fell seams. I ended with a blanket that measured 54 × 87 in. This size would make a quilt that would be narrower and longer than the average twin-size quilt, but I wanted it long enough to tuck under at the foot of the bed as this lightweight quilt would replace a sheet in the wintertime. You can make your lightweight quilt to suit your own needs, but I wouldn't advise making it any narrower in width than 54 in.

Fig. 18-1. Five old blankets.

Fig. 18-2. The first three of the five new quilts.

The size of my repaired blanket became the size of my finished quilt. I now set about making a backing for my quilt to suit the blanket size. Since the flannel I had bought was 45 in. wide, two widths sewn together would give me a length of 90 in. minus about 1 in. which would be taken up with the crosswise seam. Using two widths of my flannel to give me the length I needed for my backing certainly seemed the practical way to go about it. So I cut off two pieces of flannel, each 56 in. long. (In my finished quilt, this 56 in. would become my quilt *width*.) I sewed these two pieces together along their selvedges, using flat fell seams for extra strength. (If you are not acquainted with flat fell seams, stitch this seam twice.) With this sewing I now had a piece of flannel for my quilt backing that measured approximately 56 × 89 in. About 3¼ yards of material were required.

I laid the flannel backing on the floor *wrong side up*. When I laid the blanket on top of it, I had 1 in. of the flannel backing extending all around, ends and sides, which was exactly what I needed for finishing my quilt. In other words, the flannel backing was 2 in. wider and 2 in. longer than the blanket.

Starting at the top end, I folded down ½ in. of the raw edge of the flannel backing. I folded another ½ in. to completely hide that raw edge, and pinned the resultant "binding" down against the plaid blanket. I continued in this fashion all across the top, folding and pinning in place the flannel edge that would bind the two pieces of fabric, flannel and blanket, together. When I had pinned this "binding" (which was about ½ in. wide) in place at the top, I took it to the machine and sewed it down. Then I put it on the floor again and, in the same way, pinned in place the right side of the quilt. I sewed that. Next I went to the left side, pinning and sewing. Then I did the bottom end of the quilt. (Steam pressing your pinned binding before sewing may help to shrink it to a better fit.)

Now that the two pieces had been bound together I had to secure them with either quilting or tying. When one wants to make a quilt quickly, one usually ties it but, with this lightweight covering, I decided to quilt—on the machine.

I made five evenly spaced lengthwise stitchings on my quilt. Then I turned the whole thing sideways and made 11 evenly spaced crosswise stitchings, resulting in a rectangular pattern of machine quilting. And my quilt was done.

This quickly made quilt was a satisfying project because it was pleasant to put back into good service a blanket that might have been thrown away.

THE ENVELOPE QUILT

I had several old blankets; I couldn't stop now. Quilt number two as shown in Fig. 18-2 was a completely covered blanket and, excluding the tying of it, it was made in half a day. Besides being fast to make, it was economical because I was fortunate enough to discover another bargain in 45 in. wide material. Ordinarily, when covering an old blanket as I have done here, you would need to buy 10 yards of 36 in. wide material in order to make a quilt that will be, when finished, about 70 × 89 in. You would take the 10 yards and cut it into four 2½ yard lengths and sew two lengths together for the front covering and the other two lengths together for the back.

But when I happened on the 45 in. wide material in a mill-end outlet, I saw how I could do it another way and save yardage. Using the material crosswise as in quilt number one, instead of lengthwise, I needed to buy only 8 yards. It was an attractive drapery fabric never intended for a quilt but, at 50 cents a yard, I could not pass it by. So my pretty blue and white quilt tied with blue yarn cost me only $4 plus 77 cents for a 2 ounce skein of yarn (1 ounce would have done the tying). Even so, let me add, if the material of your choice should be the 36 in. width, go ahead and buy it. You will still be far ahead in warmth and dollars.

I've already explained briefly how to use fabric to make a covering from 36 in. material: make lengthwise seams. To make a quilt covering from 45 in. material go about it like this:

Quilt Back and Front

Lay your fabric on the floor and cut the 8 yards into four equal pieces. In pairs, then, sew the pieces together with crosswise seams to make a front and back cover for your blanket. (The seams will be along the selvedge of the material. The quilt, when finished, will have seams running crosswise along the middle, front and back, as compared with the lengthwise seams used with 36 in. material.)

After making your seams, press them to one side and continue pressing the entire quilt covering, front and back.

Quilt Filling

For the filling between my quilt cover, I used an old blue and white checked double blanket. It was worn and very thin in places but, since it was a double blanket and had to be shortened to the length of the quilt covering (about 89 in.), I used the piece I cut off the end to pad the thin areas.

To patch these areas I merely sewed, with a long machine stitch, a piece of the cutoff end to the thin places. I did not finish the patches by turning under the raw edges because they would not be seen and the material did not fray.

Assembling

After the patching (if you, too, should find it necessary), lay out on the floor one of the pieces of your quilt cover, *right side up*. On top of it lay the other piece, *wrong side up*. On top of those two pieces lay your blanket filler. Trim the edges of all three quilt parts to the same size. Now sew three of the sides to make a sort of envelope like this:

Pin together the top edge of the three thicknesses of your quilt, take it to your machine, and stitch with a ½ in. seam. Lay the quilt on the floor again, and pin it along the right side. Sew that right side with a ½ in. seam. Pin and seam the left side. Now turn it like a pillowcase so that the blanket is inside its front and back covering.

To finish the bottom edge of the quilt, lay it on the floor again and turn to the inside 1 in. of the bottom edge, front and back, including the blanket. Pin it in place. Press. Machine topstitch ½ in. from bottom edge with thread in an appropriate color, holding in any fullness while stitching. Again press that edge as well as the other three edges. Topstitch the other three edges as you did the bottom edge, and your quilt is complete except for tying it with yarn.

Tying

For tying, ideally one would have a set of quilt frames, but I do not know many people who have. If you don't have them, spread your finished quilt on the floor again and measure it. My finished quilt, after trimming it to fit the blanket width, was about 65 × 87 in. I tied my quilt every 5 in. To find out where to tie it, divide your length and width by five. The width of my quilt, 65 in., was easily divisible by five so, going across my quilt, I had rows of 12 ties alternated by rows of 13 ties. The reason for the variation is that the ties in row number two will not come directly beneath those in row number one, but instead will come between two ties in the row above. So in my case, I started my first row of tying 5 in. from the left edge, but when I started my second row I started 2½ in. from that edge. After that I tied a knot every 5 in. the rest of the way across the quilt.

But you still can't start tying without doing a bit more arithmetic. I had to find my starting point at the top left side of the quilt by dividing my length by five. I found that dividing 87 by five gave me 17 with 2 in. left over. I took care of those extra 2 in. by starting 6 in. down from the top instead of 5 in. down, and ending 6 in. from the bottom. But between the starting and ending points the rows were all 5 in. apart.

So after doing my arithmetic, I started my first tie at a point that was 6 in. down from the top and 5 in. in from the left side. Measuring down and in from the side, I made a pencil mark for my first tie. Then every 5 in. I made another pencil mark all across the width of my quilt top for the first row of ties. Row two, of course, started 2½ in. from the left side and ended 2½ in. from the right side, but all in between the ties were 5 in. apart.

Using a darning needle with a long eye and three-ply yarn in an appropriate color, I made ties at each pencil mark and cut the ends off to about 1 in. in length. I used my yarn double. Tying on the floor will assure a neat job because you are in a position to keep patting your quilt in place as you work. As you progress with your tying, you may find it helpful to roll the width of your quilt toward you.

You will be surprised to find how warm this quilt will be with only an old thin blanket in it for filling.

THE COVERED QUILT

For the filling in quilt number three I used the old quilt pictured in Fig. 18-1. The size of the end product was determined by a ready-made quilt top I found in a department store. I do not know if these "quilt ends" (as they were called) are occasionally available or if it was a one-time piece of good luck I ran into, but what I found was a whole tableful of ends of machine-made quilts for $2.22 each. They were bound around the edges and might have made a lightweight covering as they were. However, I ripped off the binding and used the "quilt end" for a quilt top of my own, even though the size was only 52 × 76 in. The "blocks" you see in the picture of Fig. 18-2 are not sewn together but are in the fabric, so one can make this same quilt by buying enough block design fabric (or any print) and following the directions for putting together the top, for filling it with an old quilt or blanket, and for using material for the back of the quilt.

Quilt Filling

Since the size of my quilt was already determined by the size of the quilt end I had bought, I cut my old quilt filler to the same size as my quilt end (which has now become my quilt *top*). I also squared off the rounded corners of the old quilt; you may not have to do this. I had already bought some plain colored blue material to harmonize with the blues and reds of my bought quilt top, so I made a back for my quilt.

Quilt Back

The blue material was 36 in. wide, so I needed to buy 4½ yards of it to make a quilt that would be 76 in. long when finished. I cut my $4^1{}_2$ yards in half crosswise so that each piece was 2¼ yards long. Then I seamed these two long pieces of fabric together lengthwise and, for firmness, stitched that seam again.

I pressed open the center seam and laid my quilt back on the floor, *wrong side up*. On top of that went my old quilt filling and then my quilt top. My quilt back was a few inches too wide, so I had to cut off the material, sides and ends, so that only 1¼ in. of fabric extended all around.

Assembling

Because the three thicknesses of the quilt were bulky, I found it helpful to pin them together about 2 in. down from the top edge before I began my "binding."

Then with my materials held securely in place, I began as before to turn under ½ in. of the extended back edge and then another ½ in. down against the front of the quilt. I pinned this $^1{}_2$ in. binding down all across the top edge; then I took it to the machine and sewed it in place. I did the right side in the same way, just as described in the directions for "Machine Quilted Lightweight Quilt." When all the sides had been "bound," I was ready to tie all those thicknesses in place. For this I used wool yarn and tied it at the corners of all the blocks in the fabric. If your fabric should not have blocks to guide your tying, tie every 4 or 5 in. and alternate the rows of ties according to the directions given for the envelope quilt.

This quilt turned out to be the warmest of all the quilts I made, and it was my daughter's favorite for that reason.

THE DIAGONAL DESIGN QUILT

After making three quilts you might have thought I would have stopped, but no—I was just getting underway. I still had too many fabrics stored in drawers and closets that I could put to use for winter warmth. This "diagonal" design is probably the simplest of block patterns one could make; nevertheless, it turned out to be one of the most attractive of the five quilts.

The Quilt Top

To get ready to make this quilt, gather all your materials and put them in piles according to colors. If you are using clothing discards, you can probably get enough blocks from about eight adult-size dresses. Though I dislike to mix old and new fabrics, I did so in this quilt, using firm, unfaded discards as well as pieces of new material.

To begin cutting your blocks, make a 5 in. square cardboard pattern. For best results, carefully cut out one block at a time. (Note: save smaller scraps for smaller blocks for another quilt—perhaps for a child's bedroom or for the little girl's skirt shown in Chapter 2.

Your finished quilt will measure about 64 × 80 in. and will be 16 blocks wide and 20 blocks long. If you want to make a larger or smaller quilt, add or subtract a block from the width and length. If you change the size of the quilt top, bear in mind that you will have to alter the size of your quilt back and blanket filling accordingly.

In the main I had about eight colors, mostly prints but also a few plain colors in brown, red, white (with blue polka dots), light blue, yellow, green, fuchsia, and dark blue.

After cutting some blocks from all your colors, arrange them in a line lengthwise on the floor or bed. Plan this 20 block row so that the colors and patterns of your fabrics complement each other. When you have laid out blocks in all your colors (eight in my case), start over again proceeding in the same sequence as before until you have laid out 20 blocks. Then sew the row together with ½ in. seams. This line of blocks will become the first row along the left edge of your finished quilt. (To save heating your iron, make several rows before pressing the seams open.)

To plan so that your blocks march across your quilt in a diagonal color stream (Fig. 18-3), start laying out your second row with the same color block that ended your first row. Then

Fig. 18-3. For a diagonal color stream, start laying out your second row with the same color block that ended your first row. The second block in the second row will be the same as the top block in the first row. The third block in the second row will be the same as the second block in the first row, etc.

proceed with this second row by making the second block in the row the same as the top block in the first row. Your third block in the second row will be the same as the second block in the first row, etc. When you have made several rows, press the seams open. You are now ready to sew the rows together, but before you do, lay them all out on the bed again to be sure that your blocks have been sewn together in the proper sequence to present the planned diagonal design. After checking, sew the rows together, being careful to see that all the corners come together exactly.

As you proceed with your sewing, undoubtedly you will have to make some pattern and even color substitutions. When you run out of a pattern, make a substitution in a similar color. If this is not possible, then stop with your scarce color at the bottom of the quilt top and start with a new color at the top of the next row. For the sake of your design, always look ahead, keeping an eye on those colors that are scarce so that you can plan what to do when each one is gone. Don't hesitate to piece material to give yourself a needed block. After all the rows have been sewn together, press the lengthwise seams open.

Quilt Back

For the back of my quilt I might have bought a nice cotton or synthetic print. However, I still had plenty of that good-quality flannel I had bought on sale, so I used that and I was pleased with the end result. The quilt was both warm to sleep under and lovely to look at.

As mentioned at the beginning of this chapter, this flannel was 45 in. wide. If you buy material of this width and make the back of your quilt with a seam down the length of it, as I did with this particular quilt of mine, you will need to buy 4⅔ yards of material.

Cut your 4⅔ yards in half crosswise so that you will have two pieces each 2⅓ yards long. Use one of these pieces full width (45 in.), but the second piece cut in half, lengthwise down the fold of the material, and use only a half width (22½ in.). By sewing the full width to the half-width with a lengthwise seam, you will have a backing for your quilt which will be about 66½ × 84 in. This manner of making your quilt back will give you a seam that runs down only one side of your material. In order to give your quilt back a more balanced effect, turn it to the wrong side and take another small seam at the same distance from the edge on the opposite side.

Note: I made my quilt back this way because there was a pretty border on the flannel that I wanted to run down either side of the back of the quilt. If you have a good use for the half-width of material cut off one side of the back, you may wish to make your back the same way. If not, it may be that you would rather make it according to the directions given for the "lightweight" and the "envelope" quilts, which is to sew your 45 in. material crosswise. This method takes only 4 yards of material.

With your quilt top and back made, let's turn our attention for a moment to the filler.

Quilt Filling

First lay out on the floor the blanket you will use as filling for your quilt and trim it to the same size as your quilt top, which should be the correct size as finished. I had some patching to do on the old green blanket I used, so I merely stitched in place a piece of plaid blanket left over from the filling of another quilt (Fig. 18-4). As mentioned before, I used a long stitch on the sewing machine and did not bother to turn under the raw edges. Another problem I had was with rippling along the edges of this old blanket. I corrected this by cutting out V-shapes to flatten those edges. When your blanket filling is in shape, you can finish putting your quilt together.

Assembling

Lay your quilt back on the floor, *wrong side up.* Lay your blanket filling on top of that. Lay your quilt top on the other two pieces. Your quilt back then will extend about an inch on all sides beyond the other two pieces. Now form a "binding" as we have done before by turning under ½ in. of the back extension and then another ½ in. against the quilt top. Pin it in

Fig. 18-4. Patched blanket filler.

place, and then sew it in place all across the top of the quilt. Continue by pinning a "binding" on the right edge of the quilt. Sew it in place. Do the same at the left edge. Then do the bottom of the quilt.

Your quilt is finished now except for tying. Using three-ply yarn and a darning needle with a long eye, tie a double knot at the corner of each block and cut the ends to about 1 in. in length. For a pieced quilt made with blocks it didn't take long to make—and isn't it pretty?

STRIP-BLOCK QUILT

While engaged in looking for materials for the "diagonal design" quilt, I ran across a surprising amount of quilted fabrics, both new and used, among my sewing scraps. Two of the fabrics were remnants from sewing projects, and the other two fabrics were from two sets of lounging pajamas which, much as I enjoy wearing such lovely gifts, seemed to have scarcely lost their newness though they must have hung in the closet for more than five years. So again I mixed new and old and felt happy doing so (Fig. 18-5), otherwise I would have had no use for those materials.

Quilt Top

In order to determine in a rough manner whether I had enough material to make a quilt top, I laid out my fabrics on

Fig. 18-5. The last two of the five new quilts.

the small-size "covered quilt" described earlier. That quilt measured 52 × 76 in. I decided that I had material enough if I could design a top that would utilize large pieces, mainly cut lengthwise. Cutting material into blocks and sewing it back together again is a waste of fabric if you have large pieces to start with.

My largest piece was a green remnant left from a coat lining, the main portion of which measured 24 × 42 in. Cutting this piece would have represented a great waste, so this became the middle of my quilt top. The next move was to design around this middle to best utilize the rest of my material. Finished, I planned that it would measure approximately the size of the "covered quilt." As it turned out I had enough fabric to make it a bit larger. The strip-block quilt, when finished, was 54 × 78 in. To make your quilt larger, you can start with a larger center rectangle.

The strip-blocks were made from pieces of material sewn together lengthwise. Two of these rather large strip blocks were needed to extend the length of the quilt at both ends, and two were needed to extend the width at each side. The corners were filled in after that with small strip blocks.

To make the two strip blocks for each end of your rectangle, cut strips from all your materials in random widths of from 2 to 5 in. The length of these strips will be 20 in. when the block is finished, but cut all strips a bit longer than that, especially when making use of old fabrics since they may have a tendency to pull up or to stretch. Sew your strips together until you have the proper width to fit one end of your center rectangle (24 in. in my case). If your finished strip block turns out to be a bit too wide to fit on the end of the rectangle, you can easily make it fit by taking a small seam down the reverse side of one of the wider strips.

You will see by the picture that I outlined both my end and my large side strip blocks by beginning and ending those strip blocks with a 2 in. wide strip of the same material used for the center rectangle. This outlining trick ties together the fabric of the center rectangle with the rest of the quilt but is not essential if you don't have enough material. On the other hand, if you have more than enough material for this trick you may wish to mix in that material with all the other materials in the strip blocks instead of only outlining them as I did. The preference is yours because the end design will be yours.

When you have finished sewing together the strips to make your end strip blocks, trim them to 20 in. in length, press the seams open, and sew the block to one end of your center rectangle. Make a second strip block in the same way, press it, and sew it to the opposite end of the rectangular center.

The two large strip blocks for the sides of the quilt were made from pieces of all materials in random widths of from 2 in. to an occasional 12 in. strip and, as mentioned before, these strip blocks like the end ones were begun and finished with a 2 in. strip of the same material as the center rectangle (or, if your prefer, you will mix that material along with the other strips in the strip block instead of outlining). All strips in the two side blocks were 16 in. long when finished but were cut perhaps an inch longer than that and then trimmed to the correct length (16 in.) when the entire block had been sewn together.

When your side strip blocks are finished, press the seams open but do *not* yet sew them to the sides of your center rectangle. Before you do that you must complete your quilt sides by making four small strip blocks for each corner of your quilt (or 16 small strip blocks in all).

For these corner strip blocks you can utilize smaller pieces of material because these small blocks, when trimmed, will measure $8\frac{1}{2} \times 10\frac{1}{2}$ in. (but don't neglect to cut them a bit longer than required and then to trim them to that measurement). All these small corner strip blocks measure the same; however, you must make eight of the 16 blocks with the strips running lengthwise and make the other eight with the strips running crosswise. (A look at Fig. 18-6 will show that these lengthwise and crosswise strip blocks are sewn together at right angles to each other to make the corners of the quilt.)

After you have made eight strip blocks with the strips running lengthwise and eight more with the strips running crosswise, press all the seams open. But do not join them together yet. Instead lay your complete center section on the floor or bed and next to it lay your side sections. Now fill in the corners, switching the small strip blocks from here to there until you find the most attractive arrangement for them. When finding the most attractive arrangement for your corner pieces, remember to place the corner strip blocks in exactly the same position in each of the four corners (Fig. 18-6). To do this you will start your first corner with a crosswise strip block in an upper lefthand position against the side section of the quilt, so you will make all your other corners with a crosswise strip block in an upper left hand position against a side section.

Press the seams, and sew the four sections together to make your completed corner pieces. Now you can sew your corner pieces to your large side strip blocks. Then join the sides of your quilt to the center piece, and your top is finished.

Fig. 18-6. Start your first corner with a crosswise strip-block in an upper left-hand position against the side section of the quilt. Make all your other corners with a crosswise strip-block in an upper left-hand position against a side section.

Filling and Quilt Back

An old rose-colored blanket became the filler for my quilt and, since it was too wide, I cut off the side of it and used that to pad a thin area through the middle merely by stitching with a long stitch to hold the patch in place. As mentioned previously, I did not trouble to turn under the raw edges of the patch because the edges would not fray and the patch would be held more securely in place later by tying the quilt. For the back of my quilt I used an old pink bedspread that was still in good condition.

Assembling

I laid the bedspread out on the floor, *wrong side up*, put my repaired blanket on top of it, and then on those two pieces placed my quilt top, *right side up*. I trimmed all pieces to the same size because to finish this quilt I would bind the three parts of it together with a separate binding.

But before binding the parts together, first stitch them. Lay them on the floor, and securely pin all three parts together at the upper end. Stitch across this end with a ½ in. seam and a long machine stitch. Pin it along the right side, and sew that together with a ½ in. seam. Next do the left side in the same way and then the bottom of the quilt.

Binding

For the separate binding you can buy blanket binding if you like, but I made mine. I cut strips of leftover material 2½ in. wide and in varying lengths of from 6 in. to an occasional 36 in. Even so, I still did not have quite enough material to go around my quilt, so I bought ¼ yard of green and ¼ yard of pink, the predominant colors in my quilt, and I cut these materials into more 2½ in. wide strips. Then, to make my binding, I sewed all the strips together, alternating colors and patterns.

Bought binding will give directions for application. If you make yours as I did, follow these directions for applying it to the quilt. Press open the seams of the joined strips of material that make your binding. Also press down ½ in. along one of the long edges of the binding. Then, with the right side of the binding to the back side of the quilt, sew the binding all along the four sides, joining the ends of the binding where they meet.

Starting at the top of the quilt, bring the binding over onto the front of the quilt and pin it in place. Keep pinning the wide binding in place until you have turned the corner at the right side of the quilt. Miter that corner as shown in Fig. 18-7. If your quilt isn't too bulky to handle, steam press this edge and mitered corner (it will help control fullness when sewing the binding). Stitch this top edge and corner on the machine. Bring it back to the floor and pin in place the binding on the right side of the quilt, turning the corner at the bottom of the quilt. Miter that corner. Press and sew. Continue in this manner the rest of the way around the quilt.

Tying

Now your quilt is all done except for tying. I decided to tie 5 in. apart. You may like to tie closer together, perhaps 3 or 4 in. apart. When you have decided on the distance between ties, measure your quilt length and width and divide by that number of inches (in my case 5 in.) to find your starting point for tying. My quilt measured 54 × 78 in. Had the width been 55 in., I would have begun my tying exactly 5 in. from the left edge of my quilt and continued tying a knot every 5 in. across the width of the quilt, ending 5 in. from the right edge. However, I lacked an inch. So instead I began tying 4½ in. from the left edge and ended 4½ in. from the right edge. But all in between I made my ties 5 in. apart.

After determining the starting point for the width of my quilt. I had to find the starting point for the length and make the two points coincide. In order to find this exact starting point, I had to divide my length by five again. I divided 78 by

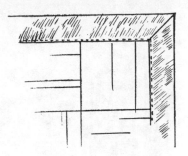

Fig. 18-7. To miter, make a concealed fold when sewing down the binding so that the result will be a neat diagonal line at each corner.

five and found I would have 15 lengthwise ties, but left over were an extra 3 in. to take into account. So instead of starting 5 in. down from the top and ending 5 in. from the bottom, as I would have if my quilt had measured 75 in., I added an extra $1\frac{1}{2}$ in. to the top and bottom tying points so that I would start my tying $6\frac{1}{2}$ in. down from the top and end $6\frac{1}{2}$ in. from the bottom. But all in between my ties would be 5 in. apart. So my exact starting point was $6\frac{1}{2}$ in. down from the top and $4\frac{1}{2}$ in. in from the left side.

The second row of ties would not be the same as the first row because ties do not come one below the other but instead alternate so that the ties on the second row come at a point halfway between the ties on the first row. Lengthwise, the ties in the second row will be 5 in. below the ties in the first row, but crosswise they will start at a point 7 in. from the left edge. If that seems too much space without a tie, then start 5 in. down and 2 in. from the left edge. The ties will end either 7 in. or 2 in. from the right edge of the quilt, but all in between they will be 5 in. apart.

Again, three-ply yarn and a darning needle will do the tying, and a 1 ounce skein is enough if you can find such a small amount.

This bonus quilt made from throw-away scraps turned out to be so beautiful that I decided to use it for a spread on a small bed.

 # Sewing For Men

This chapter got started because of a story told to me by a friend who owns a drapery shop. It was just at closing time a few years ago when a young man came in and asked to see some drapery fabric. He found some he liked and bought 26 yards. Since he was alone, she decided that he must be buying it for a bachelor apartment, so she suggested that if he needed help she had seamstresses who could help him. "Oh, no thank you," he replied, "I've made them before."

My friend was a bit apprehensive about the somewhat precise pleating arrangement that goes into most livingroom draperies, so she persisted, "If you should have any trouble with the pleating, just let me know and someone will help you."

"Oh, that's no trouble," the young man claimed, "I just staple in the pleats when I staple the draperies to the wall over the windows." Of course today many men are openly doing what used to be considered "women's work."

But at the time this story convulsed my friend, and I confess I laughed, too. However, after I thought about it, I realized that there must be a lot of men who made curtains. After all, my neighbor, a married man with a wife and two daughters, had been making curtains for their home for years and had just recently finished new ones for their kitchen.

Sure enough, in no time at all I found a young man, a biology teacher from Newark, Delaware, who does a great deal of sewing. At the time I met him he had just finished making himself a quilted ski jacket (from a kit) and had plans for making a sleeping bag and, after that, perhaps a tent. He also had made curtains for his apartment, and here are Bill's directions.

SWAG CURTAIN

Bill made the simple swag curtain shown in Fig. 19-1 for his study. To estimate the yardage for your own windows, measure across the top and down both sides of your window frame, and then add an extra yard to that length. Fabric 36 in. wide is about right.

Bill made his own tiebacks from the curtain fabric, but he had some good suggestions for alternatives: Buy metal tiebacks and secure them at the upper corners to hold the curtains, or use hoops (festoon rings) at the upper corners to run your swags through. The hoop Bill favored was one made of rope such as one might find in a ring toss game. This hoop could be covered with material or left as is. He could even have bought his own rope and made his own hoops, securing the cut ends by binding them together round and round with twine. To conceal the bound ends, secure the hoops to the wall or window frame in such a manner as to cover them with the curtain fabric when the curtains are hung.

Your material can be sheer or heavy, but whatever it is, make sure that it lends itself to gentle folds. Bill says to look carefully at your material for another reason. Like most of us, he was looking for a bargain, so he bought his lovely material at a mill end store, priced temptingly at 99 cents a yard. It wasn't until he returned home that he discovered a flaw running down the full length of the fold of the material. So if

Fig. 19-1. Swag curtain.

you are buying marked-down fabric, be sure to check for flaws. Bill proceeded to make his curtain anyway and, as he had hoped, with the curtain's many folds the flaw did not show.

Before making your curtain, cut your tiebacks from one end of your material. Cutting the tiebacks crosswise will take only about half a yard off the length of your material. Cut two strips, each 20 in. long by 8½ in. wide. Also cut two strips of interfacing 20 in. long by 4¼ in. wide. Fold one of the tieback strips of material together lengthwise, right sides together, and place a strip of interfacing on top of it. With ½ in. seams, sew the tieback and the interfacing together by stitching across one end and down the length of the open side. Trim the interfacing close to the stitching. Turn and press. Turn to the inside ½ in. of the remaining open end and stitch across it. Make the second tieback. Press both. If desired, sew two strips of bias tape trim in a color to harmonize with the fabric down the length of either side of both tiebacks and ½ in. in from their outer edges. Stitch both edges of the tape in place with a matching thread.

Now narrowly hem both long sides of your remaining material to make your swag curtain. When you have finished, get a couple of thumbtacks (this curtain requires no curtain rods) and hang your curtain by gathering it into your tiebacks and tacking them in place at each upper corner of the window frame. Make sure that the upper edge of your curtain is straight across the top of your window. Beneath the straight upper edge, arrange the folds attractively, and then ascertain how much you will need to cut off the bottom ends on each side in order to have your curtain come to the sill after narrowly hemming.

To do this make a mark with a piece of chalk at the outer edges of both ends of your curtain, allowing for a narrow hem. Take your curtain down, and spread it on a table for cutting. Cut off the ends diagonally from your chalk marks at the outer edges to a point 8 to 12 in. higher on the inner edges (see Fig. 19-2). Bill cut his curtains off at about 8 in., which made them appear almost straight across. For a cascade effect, cut them off at about 12 in. up on the inner edges (Fig. 19-3).

Gather the curtains into tiebacks again, and hang them to see if they are right for hemming. While you are about it, mark roughly with your chalk where the tiebacks hold your curtains (diagonally) at the corners to guide you in tacking your folds in place later. Take down the curtains and lay them on the table. Arrange deep folds (of about 4 in.), and with a needle and thread loosely tack the folds in place at the corners where you have marked them (the tacking will be hidden by the

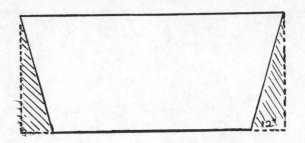

Fig. 19-2. Cut off the ends diagonally from your chalk marks.

tiebacks). Hem your swag narrowly, press it, and hang it the final time. Bill bought decorative thumbtacks to match the color of his curtains.

RUFFLE CURTAIN

The ruffle curtain shown in Fig. 19-4 seemed to fill Bill's need for sunlight in his kitchen better than anything else he could think of. Besides, it makes a very attractive window and probably costs less than any other type of curtain one could make. It would suit other rooms as well as the kitchen. I made one for my daughter's bedroom.

Bill went back to the mill end store and bought this nice crisp cotton blend for 50 cents a yard. It had a scorched selvedge which he trimmed off, but the rest of the fabric was firm and attractive.

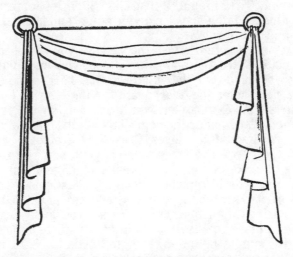

Fig. 19-3. For a cascade effect, cut them off at about 12 in. up on the inner edges.

Fig. 19-4. Ruffle curtain.

Bill's material was 36 in. wide, and that made figuring yardage easy because the ruffle was 12 in. wide. To make this curtain, measure the width of the top of your window and the length of the two sides down to the bottom of your windowsill. Bill's window, when the three sides were added together, measured 120 in. However, that amount is not what Bill bought. Because each yard would be cut into three 12 in. strips, he divided by three and got 40 in. This was the amount of material that would go around the three sides of his window once, but he needed fullness to make a ruffle, so he doubled that amount. That means Bill needed 80 in. of material or, changing inches into yards, he divided by 36 and found that 2¼ yards would do nicely.

When you have figured out the yardage you will need, that is, the length of the top and sides of your window divided by three and doubled, cut that material into 12 in. wide strips. With the right sides together, seam the three strips together with ½ in. seams to make one continuous long strip. Press the seams open. Turn under the edges on both the sides and ends and narrowly hem all the edges. Press the curtain.

Turn the curtain to the wrong side and sew two rows of bias tape to make two casings through which you will thread either ¼ in. elastic or narrow tape. (Elastic is nice, but because of its stretching it takes a longer time to thread through casings than tape does.) To aid you in sewing your bias tape in place, measure 5 in. in from your hemmed edge toward the middle of the curtain and make a mark with a pencil. Measure from the opposite side and make a mark. Do this measuring and marking, 5 in. from both sides, the entire length of the curtain. These pencil marks will guide you in sewing your bias tape in place.

Begin sewing by folding under the raw end of the tape and laying it on the material ¼ in. above the hem in the end of the ruffle. Sew from pencil mark to pencil mark, keeping a ruler at hand to make sure that the inside edge of your tape is 5 in. from the edge of the curtain. When it is finished you will have sewn two rows of tape along the two rows of pencil marks so that there will be an inch separation down the middle of the curtain between the two rows of tape.

After sewing both casings in place, cut a piece of ¼ in. elastic about the length of the three sides of your window (if you are using tape, cut a bit more than twice that amount). With a safety pin attached to the end of your elastic or tape, run it through the two casings in one continuous thread. Then tack the ends together where they meet.

This will leave a loop at each end of your curtain ¼ in. above the bottom hemline. Anchor those loops with two thumbtacks stuck into your window sill on either side of your window. (The four thumbtacks will be hidden by the bottom hems.) Now with two more thumbtacks secure the top corners. If you press the thumbtacks into the top of the upper frame, they will be out of sight. Put one more thumbtack in the middle of the top of the frame (out of sight), and your attractive curtain has been hung—and without the need for rods.

EASY PANELS

Figure 19-5 shows a kind of curtain familiar to all of us—and it was to Bill. He had made them for different rooms in apartments he had lived in because this style of curtain goes anywhere.

In this case, however, I am not showing Bill's panels. I am showing my own because the reader may be interested in the fact that the material I used was lingerie fabric.

I had been making lingerie from nylon fabrics using a sheer chiffon when the idea came to me. "I wonder if this would work," I said, holding the folds of the lovely pale blue material up to my kitchen window. The material came in a width of 180 in. By cutting that width in half, I could make two curtains, each 54 in. wide, by buying just the length of my window plus enough more for hems at the top and bottom. I found that 1½ yards would make curtains for one window.

To figure the amount of material I needed for one window, I added to the length of the window 3 in. for a top hem and 12 in. for a bottom hem. This amount would not only take care of the wide hems I planned at the bottom, but would allow for

Fig. 19-5. Panel curtain.

trimming in case of any unevenness in the material due to careless cutting.

I cut my material in half to make my two 54 in. panels. I narrowly hemmed the side edges of each curtain. Then I turned down a 3 in. hem at the top and stitched it down. About 1½ in. up from that stitching, I made a casing for my curtain rod by sewing another row of stitching across the top of the curtain parallel with the first stitching. (The width of your casing will depend upon the width of your curtain rod.)

The top hem and casing is made so that, after the curtain is strung on the rod, there will be a little ruffle at the top. It is a good idea to hang your curtains before putting in the bottom hem. This way you can see whether the curtains need a little trimming with scissors to even the bottoms. I made my hems wide (7 in.) because I thought wide hems would look attractive in the sheer material.

Here are a few words about sewing on nylon chiffon if you have never worked with it before: It is best to buy a ballpoint needle and polyester thread. (It is not much of a trick to change needles.) Use a rather long stitch when sewing, and hold your material firmly, before and behind the needle, but do not stretch it. You may have to adjust your tension a little. Your beautiful and economical curtains will be worth the little extra trouble. You'll find this gorgeous fabric sheds dirt, stays lovely longer and, when the time comes, washes like a dream. Press *carefully* (if at all) with an iron that is barely warm.

What to Do With Fabric Scraps and Glue

Although the projects in this chapter do not require any sewing to complete, it seemed only right to include them because they provide a means for using up scraps of fabric. You can even use swatches of fabric that are not much bigger than this book to make some of the items. Then, too, many of the projects would make nice gifts when an inexpensive one is called for.

The first one, a dainty paperweight, as you can see from Fig. 20-1, would make a suitable gift for any business-oriented woman from an executive to a typist. To make it you'll need a scrap of tightly woven fabric, preferably in a miniprint, one-half of a stocking egg, sewing trim, cardboard, a pipe cleaner, and plaster of Paris. Use white trim or a color coordinate with the scrap of fabric.

Invert the egg half, and place it in a small glass. Pour plaster of paris into the egg. Add water and stir until the plaster is the thickness of mayonnaise. Set this aside until the plaster hardens. Meanwhile, draw the butterfly on a double thickness of fabric. Cut it out through both thicknesses.

On cardboard, trace around only the top half of the butterfly. Cut it out. Trim the cardboard to make it slightly smaller than the fabric butterfly. Bend the pipe cleaner in half. Insert the cardboard and the bent end of the pipe cleaner between the two butterflies. Line up the outer edges of the butterflies and cardboard. Allow the pipe cleaner ends to protrude at the center top for the antennae. Glue the cardboard and bent end of the pipe cleaner between the butterflies. Do not glue the bottom wing sections together. Glue the bottom sections of the wings to the top of the egg with one wing section on each side of the egg. Glue the trim around the bottom edge of the egg.

Fig. 20-1. Pretty but practical paperweight is made from a stocking egg.

Here's a gift (Fig. 20-2) that would be appreciated by anyone who sews. To make the pincushion you'll need a jar lid 3 in. in diameter, a scrap of cotton fabric, velvet ribbon in a ½ in. width, a 3 in. Styrofoam ball cut in half, and felt squares or scraps in two shades of green.

Start by covering the Styrofoam ball half with the fabric. Pull the excess material to the underside of the ball. Tack it fast with a stapler, and insert the covered ball in the jar lid. Cut two sizes of petals from the felt. Glue the small petals of one shade to the larger petals of the other shade. Glue the petals around the jar lid.

Cut a piece of ribbon long enough to circle the jar lid, and glue it in place. Form a bow from another piece of ribbon, and glue it over the seam where the ends of the ribbon are joined.

Have you ever wondered what to do at summer's end with all those tennis ball cans? Why not put them to practical use as doorstops by weighting them down with plaster of Paris and

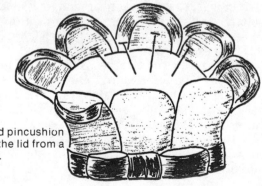

Fig. 20-2. This petaled pincushion is fashioned around the lid from a large-sized coffee jar.

Fig. 20-3. A tennis ball holder can be decorated with felt and weighted with plaster of Paris to make a handy doorstop.

covering the cans with felt? Decorate them with flowers cut from felt scraps. The results are shown in Fig. 20-3.

Mix enough plaster of Paris to fill the can at least halfway. Allow enough time for the plaster to set and harden. Then cut a felt square down to can size and glue the felt around the can. From a contrasting color of felt, cut out a scalloped border long enough to circle the can. Glue the border in place at the bottom.

Cut out four flowers and stems from the remaining scraps and glue them in place. Cut out a double-petaled flower from two shades of felt and glue it to the lid.

You also can turn a tennis ball can into a toy soldier bank like the one in Fig. 20-4. The soldier's hat calls for scraps of fake fur and hides the coin slot which is found in the lid of the can. Felt scraps in black, red, pink, white, and blue and lightweight cardboard also are needed to complete the bank.

Start out by cutting pink, red, and blue felt strips 2½ in. wide and long enough to go around the can. With the lid in place, glue the felt to the can with the pink on top, the red next, and the blue on the bottom. Cut out eyes, cheeks, a mouth, and a uniform trim from the remaining felt scraps, and glue them in place.

To make the hat, cut a piece of cardboard 2¾ in. wide and 10 in. long. Form the cardboard into a circle large enough to

Fig. 20-4. Use up your fake fur and felt scraps to turn a tennis ball can into a toy soldier bank. The coin slot is hidden by the fur hat.

slip on the can, and staple the ends. Glue the fur around the circle. Trace around the can lid on the cardboard. Add ½ in. all around. Cut out the circle and make ¼ in. wide clips in it, running from the outer edges to the inner circle, a distance of ¹₂ in. Fold the clipped edges along the lines of the inner circle. Apply glue to the top edges of the hat on the inside. Insert the cardboard circle from the opposite end of the hat, and push it through to the top. Press the clipped edges to the side of the hat. Trace around the can lid on the wrong side of the fur. Cut out the furry circle, and glue it to the top of the hat. Cut a slot in the can lid to accommodate the coins.

If you have any vinyl scraps on hand, you might want to cover a 3-pound shortening can with them and use it to hold mail or for some other purpose (Fig. 20-5). You'll also need a piece of brown wrapping paper as a base for your patchwork, because it's easier to glue the scraps to the paper first rather than to apply them directly to the sides of the can.

First measure the height and circumference of the can and cut the brown paper to that size. Cut the vinyl into pieces.

Place the wrapping paper flat on a counter top, and glue the vinyl to the paper. Overlap the pieces slightly. Press this with a heavy book for several hours; then glue the vinyl-patched paper to the can. Cut a strip of vinyl 1 in. wide and long enough to circle the can. Spread glue on the top edges of the can, on the outside. Press the bottom half of the strip in place on the glued edge. Then apply glue to the inside edges of the can at the top, and fold the remaining half of strip to the inside. Press it in place. Use spring-type clothespins to hold the strip in place until the glue dries.

A 3-pound shortening can also can be covered with ribbon (velveteen in different colors was put to work in making the ribbon-trimmed can pictured) and used in the bathroom to hold hair rollers or an extra roll of toilet tissue (Fig. 20-6). In addition to three or more shades of ribbon in a ⅝ in. width, you'll need narrow ribbon and rickrack.

First cut nine pieces of ⅝ in. width ribbon that are long enough to circle the can. Then, starting at the top, apply glue to a narrow section of the can, going completely around it. Press ribbon over the glued part, beginning and ending at the seam on the can. Continue to appy glue and to press the ribbons in place until the sides of the can are covered. You might find, as I did, that you'll have to lap the last ribbon over the one above it because of a lack of space.

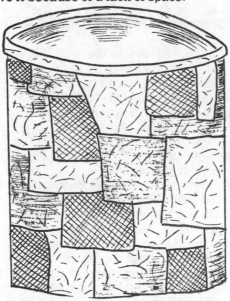

Fig. 20-5. 3-pound shortening can, vinyl-patched, can be used as a mail holder.

Fig. 20-6. Cover a large shortening can with velvet ribbon to make a holder for a spare roll of toilet tissue.

Glue rickrack or narrow ribbon over the edges of some of the ribbons. Make a bow from the leftover ribbon, and glue it to the center of the lid.

Fabric can be used, too, to dress up a 3-pound shortening can. Here's how: Cut a piece of tightly woven cotton fabric in a pretty print. Make it long enough to circle the can, and add an extra ½ in. so that you can turn the raw edge under. Make the fabric as wide as the can is high plus an extra inch. This will give you enough material to turn under the edges at the top and bottom. Turn under ½ in. at the top and bottom edges of the fabric and glue the fabric to the can. Turn the overlapping raw edge under, and glue it down.

You can line memory boxes or miniature hutches with brightly colored print cottons, too. First you'll have to play carpenter and make a sturdy box with partitions similar to the one shown in Fig. 20-7. Stain or paint it, but do not paint the bottom on the inside or outside. Then cut pieces of white cardboard or heavy white paper for each compartment in the box. Slip each piece in place to make certain that it is the exact size needed. Trim if necessary. Remove the pieces of cardboard, and trace around each one on the fabric. Cut out and glue the fabric to the corresponding pieces of cardboard.

Glue cardboard-backed fabric to the inside of the box. I lined my box, which was stained in a medium brown shade, with the same red and white gingham check I used to sew my toaster cover. The box added a cheery touch to a dark paneled wall.

An eight-sided box (mine came filled with potato chips) can be covered with fabric and turned into an attractive wastebasket. I used scraps of white pique, a black and white seersucker in a 1 in. check, a black and white print, and a white and black print to make the one shown in Fig. 20-8. It took 4 yards of ribbon to trim this particular box, which was 9½ in. tall. The yellow and white gingham check ribbon I used was a decorative way of covering the raw edges of the fabrics. This ribbon, which appeared to be made of polished cotton, was not bought in the notions section but in the hobby and crafts department.

To make this wastebasket, start by carefully cutting away the lid and flaps on the box. Then cut eight pieces of fabric that are slightly wider than the sides on the box and 4 in. longer. Turn the box on its side, and glue one strip of fabric to each side. Apply the glue to the box rather than to the fabric and pay particular attention to the corners, because it's usually harder to get the fabric to adhere to them. Allow about 2 in. of material at the top edges of the box, but don't attempt to turn the fabric to the inside or to cover the box bottom until all the strips are glued in place. When you have finished the sides, apply glue to the top and inside edges of the box and turn the strips to the inside. Press them in place. Turn the excess fabric at the bottom to the underside of the box and glue it down.

Fig. 20-7. A red and white gingham check decorates the inside of this miniature hutch.

Fig. 20-8. This wastebasket features four different fabrics—all in white or white and black prints. A ribbon trims the corners and covers raw edges of fabric.

Cut eight pieces of ribbon in the same length as the fabric strips you used to cover your box. Save the remaining ribbon to cover the ends of the fabric on the inside of the box. Glue the ribbon to the corners of the box, covering the raw edges of the fabric. Start on the inside of the box where the fabric begins and work your way over the top and down the sides. Do not glue the ribbon to the box bottom just yet. Getting the ribbon to adhere to the corners of the box can be a little tricky, but if you apply glue both to the back of the ribbon and to the corners of the box, the ribbon should go on quite nicely. Crease the ribbon slightly as you press it in place, and run your fingertips up and down it until the glue forms a bond between the fabric and ribbon. Use spring-type clothespins to hold the ribbons in place at the top edges until the glue dries. Before gluing the ribbon to the underside of the box, make a clip in the center of each ribbon, cutting close to the point where the ribbon is glued to the side of the box. Glue the remaining ribbon over the ends of the fabric on the inside of the box. Trace around the wastebasket on a piece of cardboard to make a bottom for it that will cover the raw edges of the material. Cut it out and glue it to the wastebasket bottom.

The smallest scraps of fabric plus some glue and a clear finish are all it takes to put a decorative touch on items such as the step stool shown in Fig. 20-9. For this project use fabric left from sewing kitchen curtains or another suitable scrap, preferably a print. First make a pattern from tissue paper or cardboard. (You can use the tissue from an old dress pattern.) Then either pin the tissue pattern to the fabric or trace around the cardboard to make your design. It needn't be a butterfly; a flower or piece of fruit would also be at home in the kitchen. You might find that placing the pattern on the bias of the material will give you an interesting effect.

Cut out the design, and glue it to the back of the step stool. When the glue dries, give the back of the stool a protective finish, preferably two layers, letting it dry between applications. I experimented with three different products, two in liquid form and one spray, and found that I obtained the most satisfactory results with the spray. It didn't alter the color in any way, and I tested it for resistance to spills and splashes by pouring a few drops of orange juice on fabric treated with the spray and found that the juice did not soak into it. It was easy to blot up the spill, and there were no ill effects to the fabric. The transparent protective spray I refer to is the kind used to preserve artwork. It is usually found in paint stores, shelved with the spray paints.

This same process can be used to redo a tray table by covering the inside of the tray with a patchwork made of coordinating fabrics (Fig. 20-10). If the paint is worn or chipped, you'll probably want to start off by giving the tray a fresh coat. Be sure, though, to paint the tray or that part which will be covered by fabric in a shade that is lighter than the material if the fabrics you plan to use are not completely opaque.

When the paint is dry, gather a suitable assortment of scraps and cut these into squares and rectangles. Select only fabrics which are tightly woven. And if it looks as though you're going to have problems with fraying, pink whatever edges will be exposed to view. It's helpful, too, to cut fabrics along the selvages whenever possible. The straight edges of the selvages and the pinked edges only serve to make your patchwork more interesting.

Arrange the patches on the tray, rounding off the edges of those patches in the four corners so that they conform to the shape of the tray. Spread glue evenly on the backs of the

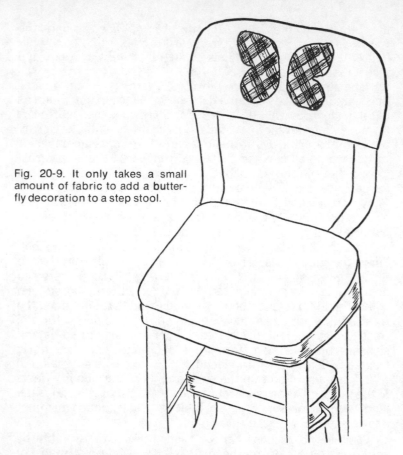

Fig. 20-9. It only takes a small amount of fabric to add a butterfly decoration to a step stool.

swatches, and glue them down. Press this with a heavy book until the glue is dry. Spray the tray with a clear finish, giving it two thin coats.

Bias strips of a cotton fabric that feature minidesigns can be used to brighten up the rims of the clay or plastic round flower pots that hold your indoor plants. To do this, first measure the width of the rim and add 1 in. to this figure. Cut a bias strip that is ½ in. longer than the circumference of the rim. Turn under ½ in. at the top and bottom and one side edge of the strip; press. Glue the strip to the rim of the pot, starting with the edge of the fabric that is not turned under.

A frilly pencil holder such as the one shown in Fig. 20-11 is sure to please anyone on your gift list. To make it you'll need to round up an empty soup can (regular size), calico scraps, rickrack, and ruffled sewing trim.

Begin the project by cutting out five 2 in. wide strips of calico from different colors and prints. Make them 4¾ in. long.

190

Fig. 20-10. Scraps of harmonizing patterns and colors were glued to a tray to get this effect.

Turn under the raw edges ½ in. at the top and bottom, and glue the strips to the sides of the can, overlapping each slightly. Glue rickrack over the raw edges of the strips. Finish by gluing ruffled sewing trim around the bottom of the can.

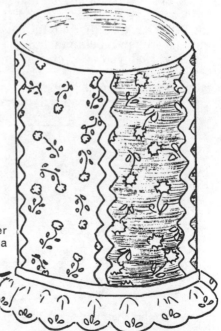

Fig. 20-11. This frilly pencil holder is made from calico scraps and a soup can.

Pretty print fabrics also can be used to cover the lids of boxes intended for use in gift giving (Fig. 20-12). The box need not then be gift wrapped, and the recipient can use it to store small items. For best results, choose a miniprint fabric to cover the lid of a small box. Select a box without any print on the bottom half or one whose sides are hidden by the top half of the box. Here's how it's done.

Set the lid on the fabric to determine how much is needed. Allow enough for turning the fabric to the inside of the box top. Cut out the fabric and center the box top on it. Apply glue to the sides of the box on the inside and outside. Turn the fabric to the inside on the long sides of the box, pressing down to secure it. At the short ends of the box, fold the material as you would when wrapping a gift with paper; then turn the fabric to the inside. Apply any extra glue necessary to the folded edge of the fabric. Secure the fabric with spring-type clothespins until the glue dries.

A length of vinyl is all that's needed to complete this next project, which is ideal for a household with a tropical fish enthusiast in it. From the vinyl, you can cut a protective cover of the desired size for a bookcase or dresser top so that you don't have to worry about drips and minor spills. Since vinyl doesn't fray, there's no need to hem it.

A dresser cover for a child's room can be made from a leftover piece of fake fur, and it also does not involve any sewing. You can either cut the cover in a free form shape or in the conventional rectangular one.

Now that you've seen what magic can be wrought with scissors and glue alone, perhaps you'll want to invent other novel uses for your scraps. Sew with them, patch with them, glue them, but don't ever toss them out!

Fig. 20-12. This charming fabric-covered box eliminates the need for gift-wrapping.

Batik—The Unusual Gift

Batik is an old art form which is believed to have originated in Indonesia nearly 2000 years ago. It became popular in the Middle Ages among the royalty, but many years passed until the common people were allowed to make use of the process for themselves.

In true batik, the designs in those early times were made with "pens" filled with hot wax. The design of the material came about as a result of the dye which penetrated the fabric every place but where the material was covered with wax.

This type of batik is still done today. However, the following instructions for batiking a tie and scarf are a modern version of the old art. You will make use of the old methods, but you also will have the advantage of crayons (colored wax). This gives you, the modern-day artist, an extra dimension and far more colors to work with. This is not to say that our designs today will be more beautiful than the old designs, because those ancient batiks were made with countless dots of wax, giving the designer hours of pleasure in shaping works of art in fabric—something that many of us do not have the time or inclination for in our hurried world. But with the added aid of colored crayons, we can shape designs different from and perhaps as lovely as those of long ago.

The result will be a tie or scarf, each costing under $5, for which you would have to pay (if you could find the item) upward of $25.

Use plain, white, natural fabrics. Then it will be up to you to design the virgin material. Give yourself plenty of time so that you can enjoy it (as a painter must enjoy the emergence of a picture on canvas). Batik should not be hurried.

The tie and scarf in Fig. 21-1 were designed with crayons and dyes. The tie was made from 100% wool and the scarf,

Fig. 21-1. The tie and scarf pictured were designed with crayons and dyes.

from pure silk. Here are the materials you will need before beginning to make a tie or scarf (I made both at the same time so that I could use the same dye baths):

Tie pattern
Fine white wool for tie
White china silk for scarf
Black dye
Brown dye (or some other background color such as rust, tan, blue, or green)
Paraffin wax and beeswax
Six small brushes (three will do if you wipe the brushes before switching colors)
One large ½ in. wide brush (for waxing large areas)
Rubber gloves
Crayons (an opportunity to use those broken ones)
Newspapers
Absorbent towels, napkins, or tissues
Six-cup muffin pan
Roasting pan or electric frying pan

Before starting work on your tie or scarf, buy ¼ yard of 100% cotton (bleached or unbleached) to practice on until you feel competent to begin work on the wool or silk. Wash, rinse, and when it is damp dry iron the cotton.

When you are finished, draw on paper the designs you will use (Fig. 21-2). Start with three ½ in. rows of triangles (trees), separated one from the other by two ⅛ in. wide spaces. Below the three rows of trees is one 2½ in. wide space to contain rectangles and squares (houses). Then there is another ⅛ in. wide space to separate the houses from the next three rows of trees.

When the model on paper suits you, start sketching with a soft lead pencil on your washed and ironed practice material. This practice is a must. You may want to use a ruler to line up the sides of your trees freehand if you like, since in "painting" them with melted wax your lines will not turn out perfectly true and straight anyway (nor is it desirable that they should, because that is part of the charm of the finished work).

Start the design on your practice material by drawing a straight line 1 in. down from the top edge of your material (be sure that edge is straight). From that line measure down ½ in. and make a pencil mark. Move your pencil and ruler and make another mark. Draw another line parallel to the first line through the two pencil marks. Now you have marked off across the width of your material a ½ in. space for your first row of trees. Make a ^{1}₈ in. space and two more ^{1}₂ in. spaces for your first row of trees. Make a ⅛ in. space and two more ½ in.

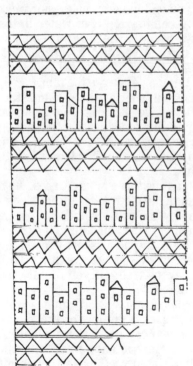

Fig. 21-2. Draw the designs you will use on paper.

spaces separated by a ⅛ in. space. In other words, you will make spaces of ½, ⅛, ½, ⅛, and ½ in.

Immediately below, rule off a space 2½ in. wide for houses and another ⅛ in. space. (This ⅛ in. space will separate the houses from the first of the next three rows of trees.) Repeat your trees and houses several times to create plenty of designs on which to practice your painting with hot wax. Fill in your spaces with trees and houses, using your paper sketch as a model.

Painting

After the designs have been sketched on your sample piece of material, cut up paraffin and put it in the six muffin cups. Add ¼ as much beeswax as paraffin to each of the cups, and then add a bit of crayon to all the cups except one. That one will remain white. My colors were yellow, green, blue, fuchsia, pink, and white. Put the muffin pan in your electric frying pan with water in the bottom and turn it to 250°. If you are working on a tabletop, pad beneath the frying pan with newspapers. Pad your work surface with newspapers, too, to protect it from wax spills.

If you use a roasting pan you will have to make your work space on your stove or nearby counter top. Put water in the roaster and turn on one or two burners. Be sure to replenish the water supply from time to time because it will boil off. When the wax is at the proper temperature, it will penetrate the fabric to the reverse side. It must penetrate the fabric.

Dip one of your small brushes in your green wax and start painting your trees. Do not begrudge the time you spend on your practice fabric; it will pay dividends in a better job on your tie or scarf. While carrying wax on your brush from muffin cup to fabric, hold a tissue or small piece of cloth beneath the brush to catch drips.

When you have finished doing the three rows of trees, dip a small brush into white wax and make a stroke on either side of the green trees. Do this by laying the brush somewhat on the tree and stroking the outside edges. This will outline the trees, making them show up better after the tie or scarf is dyed the background color. It isn't necessary to always outline both sides of the tree or to outline every tree. (If you prefer, you may omit the outlining altogether.)

You are ready to do your houses now. You can see from my sketches that each row of houses is not identical one with the other. However, if you like, you can make yours all alike. Nor are my houses colored the same in each row—with one exception. All the houses with pointed roofs have their roofs painted white and their windows painted white, but the house itself is not painted at all. This way all the houses will turn out black from the final dye. All the other houses with flat or slanted roofs are painted in colors, but their windows are not painted. These windows also will turn out black from the final dye. In other words, everything not covered with wax will turn out black in the final dye. (There will be two dyes. The first one will be the background color of the tie or scarf.)

To help you get started, let me name the colors of the top row of houses in the scarf sketched. Left to right are white, blue, yellow, uncolored (with white windows and roof), pink, fuchsia, yellow, green, uncolored (with white windows and roof), blue, green, white, pink, uncolored (with white windows and roof), white, and fuchsia. On the tie only the midportion of these houses will show, because when finished the sides of the tie will be folded under. After practice, you will be ready to begin work on your tie.

Tie

You may have to call several stores because natural fabrics are not always easy to find among today's synthetics. Buy the amount of fine white wool that your pattern recommends. (I needed ⅝ yard for a 4 in. wide tie.) When you reach home, wash the wool in lukewarm water and gentle suds, rinse it well, and hang it on a line to dry (do not use a drier). When the material reaches the damp-dry stage, press it being careful that your iron is not too hot. Washing will help pre-shrink the material, preparing it for the dyeing process (where it may shrink a bit more).

Now lay your material on a table and place your two tie sections (wide and narrow) on the material as directed in the instructions—that is, diagonally along the material. Do not cut it out. Do all your artwork and dyeing before cutting out the tie pieces. When you are very sure your tie pieces are exactly on the "straight grain" of the fabric (pat the material to make it spring into its natural shape), pin your two tie pieces in place on the wool. (Are your arrows in the pattern on the "straight grain"?) Be sure to give your pattern pieces ample room all around to take into account any more shrinkage that may take place in the dyes.

Now with your soft lead pencil, roughly outline the tie pieces so that when you remove your pattern pieces you will know where to sketch your trees and houses. Cut the material on which the tie pieces are pinned from the larger piece of wool so that you can more easily work on the tie designing.

Remove your pattern pieces and begin to mark off the ½ in. wide space for your first row of trees. Make your first line

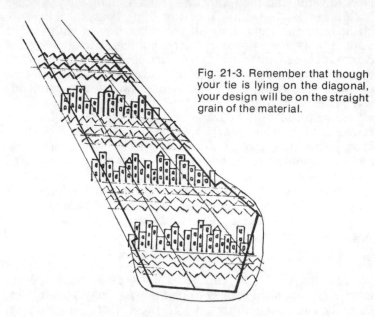

Fig. 21-3. Remember that though your tie is lying on the diagonal, your design will be on the straight grain of the material.

5½ in. down from the back neck seam on the wide tie section. (You need not batik the narrow section unless you want to.)

Remember that though your tie is lying on the diagonal (Fig. 21-3) your design will be on the *straight grain* of the material (when finished, however, the design will appear on the diagonal).

For the trees, make spaces running across your tie as you did on your practice material: ½, ⅛, ½, ⅛, ½ in. wide. For your houses make spaces 2½ and ⅛ in. Repeat until you have the needed spaces; then fill in the trees and houses. You should end about 1 in. from the bottom of the space outlined for your tie with a row of trees. Because you have outlined the shape of the tie front, you will need to design only the material needed for the tie. When the designs are finished you can begin your painting.

But first practice a bit on a scrap of the wool to get the feel of the work again and to see that the wax is at the proper temperature to penetrate the material. Start your painting of the tie at the top row so that if you make a mistake it will be in the neckline area. When moving from muffin pan to tie, remember to hold a tissue or piece of cloth beneath the brush. If you should drop a bit of wax on the tie, go on with the design. An occasional accident will not be noticed in the finished work. Sometimes you can change the design a bit to include the drop in it. If hot wax sometimes flows into windows, covering them, never mind—paint over those windows and try again on the next house.

White is a good color to use frequently because it will make the black and other colors show up better in the finished tie. Handle the waxed tie front as little as possible so that the wax on trees and houses does not become too cracked. (You will crack it deliberately later, but you won't want it so cracked that the wax will flake off the material.)

Dye Bath Number One

Prepare the dye bath of brown, green, blue, tan, or rust according to the directions on the package. Make the bath only warm. (If it is hot, it will melt the wax.) A half package will be enough, but remember to cut the amount of water as well as the dye. If you plan on making the scarf as well as the tie, a half package will dye both.

Before dipping the tie, make some sample trees and houses on a scrap of wool and dip that to see how the dye takes and to give you an idea of just how deep a color you like.

Then immerse the tie material without cutting out the tie front and back. With rubber gloves move the material around in the bath. (If you are dyeing a scarf, too, and have in mind matching the two, dye the tie first and then dip the scarf because the silk will take up the dye faster than the wool and you can better match the scarf to the tie than the other way around.) When the tie has reached a shade darker than desired, hang it on a line to dry. Do not dry it near heat because the heat will cause the wax to run into the fabric around the designs.

When the tie is dry, lay the front and back pattern pieces in place again on the dyed material. With a few pins fasten the pattern in place and cut free that part of the material where the back (narrow) tie pattern lies—unless you have batiked that section as well as the front. In that case do no cut free that part of the tie. (You will see that the wax has drawn up the material and the dye bath has shrunk it a bit, but if you have been generous in allowing material for shrinkage, you will still be able to cut out your tie.)

The Final Dye Bath

The second and final dye bath will be black. Before you dip your tie in the black dye, you must cover with wax all parts of the tie except those you want to become black. The parts you will wax (with white wax) will be the entire background color of the tie front, not forgetting that neck area of 5½ in. that was not designed (as well as the entire background color of the narrow section of the tie, *if* you batiked that section). If you did not batik the narrow section, do not immerse it in the black dye. The parts that you will not wax will be the windows of all the colored houses and those uncolored houses with pointed roofs.

When you have mixed the black dye in warm, not hot, water according to directions and are ready to immerse the tie front, do one thing more. Crumple the waxed material so that the wax cracks. This is so the black dye will run into the creases, becoming a part of your design. Now immerse the tie front and keep moving it with your hand (in a rubber glove) until all areas to be colored black are dyed.

Remove it from the dye, rinse until the water runs color-free, and once again dry it away from heat (perhaps on a line covered with old cloth with newspapers on the floor beneath).

Ironing

When the tie is damp dry, carefully press it to melt away the wax like this: Layer your ironing board with newspapers and then paper napkins, towels, or facial tissues. On top of this absorbent bed, place your tie. Cover one end of your tie with paper napkins, paper towels, or tissues, and begin to press the wax from the tie fabric. Keep removing and replacing the absorbent paper from below and above the tie as you proceed. When you have ironed the wax from the full length of the tie, go over it again in the same way to be sure you have absorbed all the wax possible. You may even find it a good thing to go over the tie a third time.

Now you are ready to lay your pattern pieces on the designed front of your tie and the dyed back (narrow) sections of your tie to cut them out. Be very sure that the arrows on the tie pieces are on the "straight of the grain."

Proceed to sew the tie according to directions. I am sure that when finished you will be as pleased with your work of art as any artist could be.

Scarf

Though the directions here will call for silk, you can make a lady's scarf of the same wool that was used for the tie, though it does not drape quite as softly. If you do make a wool scarf, cut it on the diagonal and design it on the *straight*, as the tie was done (Fig. 21-4). When the batiking is done, fringe the slanted ends of the wool scarf to about ¼ or ½ in. and stitch across above the fringes to keep the scarf from fringing further. Press down, and hem the sides by hand.

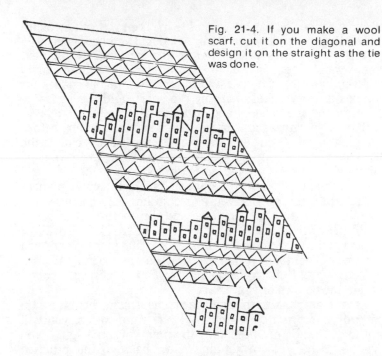

Fig. 21-4. If you make a wool scarf, cut it on the diagonal and design it on the straight as the tie was done.

For the silk scarf, buy ¼ yard of china silk. This scarf will be on the straight grain of the fabric, and the length will be determined by the width of the material unless you wish to cut it a certain length. (My silk scarves were 36 in. long.)

Pull the threads along the side edges and trim if needed. (If the clerk doesn't pull threads when you buy the material, ask her to do it so that none of the material will be wasted by careless cutting.) Press under a narrow hem along the sides and ends, and hem it on the machine with a silk thread.

Before beginning to sketch the designs on your scarf with a soft lead pencil, measure down 1 in. from the end of your hemmed scarf. Make a mark with your pencil. Move the pencil and ruler and make another mark 1 in. down from the end of your scarf. Draw a line through those two marks. Now you have your starting line for your trees and houses, which will run the full length of your scarf.

Measure down twice again from the line you just made and draw another line ½ in. from the top line. This ½ in. space you have just drawn across the width of your scarf will contain your first row of triangles (trees). As for the tie, make two more ½ in. spaces for trees, making three ½ in. spaces for trees in all. The three ½ in. spaces will be separated, one from the other, by ⅛ in. spaces. In other words, for your trees you will have spaces ½, ⅛, ½, ⅛, and ½ in. Then you will measure off for your houses a space 2½ in. wide and another space of ⅛ in. (this ⅛ in. space is to separate the houses from the next three rows of trees). A look at the sketches will help to clarify the directions. As you continue to measure off the spaces for your design down the length of the scarf, fold it lengthwise from time to time to be sure your lines are straight.

Sketch your trees and houses. Do all your sketching before beginning to paint your designs because the hot wax causes the silk to pucker, making it difficult to sketch after you have done a bit of painting. When you do begin to paint, to help control puckering, place a sheet of paper (such as typing paper) beneath the area of silk you are painting. As you move on, leave that sheet of paper in place and slip another sheet under the area you are about to begin work on. Leave all the sheets of paper in place until you have finished, folding them toward you as you work (gently so as not to crack the wax too much).

You should finish your design with a row of trees about 1 in. from the bottom of your scarf.

Let me emphasize that unless you have already made a tie and had your practice lesson on plain white cotton, you will want to do that before beginning to "paint" your design. If you have not done your practicing, turn back to the practice directions and do it now.

After that you are ready to dip your brush into hot green wax and paint your first tree on your scarf. It will be worth all the time and care you have put into it. Whether you keep it yourself or give it to someone special, you will have created a treasure.

Note: When you are finished, let the wax patties harden. Then reheat them in the roaster just enough to soften the bottom of the patties. Run your knife around the edge and lift it out. Save it for future use in batik or candle-making.

Sewing Tricks

You don't necessarily need a skirt band. Finish the raw edge of the skirt (or slacks) by binding it with a piece of wide ribbon or 1 in. wide bias tape. Cut the ribbon or tape the length of the waistline edge plus 2 in. and enclose the raw edges of the garment between the lengthwise fold of this "binding." Turn under the extra inch at each side opening edge. Now fold this bound waistline edge to the inside of the skirt far enough to hide the stitching you have just made (about ⅝ in.), and tack it here and there around the waistline to keep the finished edge from rolling out.

It's scarcely any more difficult to make an entire skirt. All you need is a piece of material about 44 to 54 in. wide and long enough for a 3 in. hem and a 2 in. turnover at the waistline. Insert elastic in the waistline turnover (casing).

If buttonholes or zippers present a problem, try small strips of adhesive closure (Velcro) to close your placket. It can be bought in several colors for about 10 cents an inch, and you merely have to topstitch two strips or two small squares in place on slacks, shorts, or children's clothing. It works well on leather, too.

Fairly long scissors are easier to work with than short ones.

If you are right-handed, cut with scissors to the right of the pattern. Lefties cut to the left. (Did you know that you can buy scissors made for lefties?)

Is the fashionable braid trim too expensive for your budget? Try a combination of rickrack and hand embroidery. Sew on rickrack and then do an "across" stitch with floss or wool diagonally over the rickrack in a contrasting color. Make two or three rows this way (Fig. 22-1).

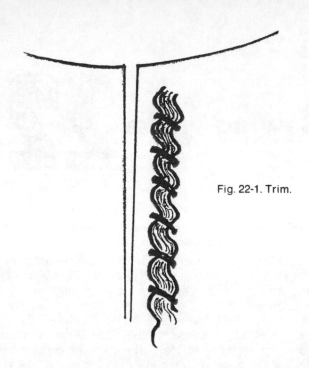

Fig. 22-1. Trim.

Do your child a favor and teach her the old-fashioned embroidery stitches so she can produce her own high-fashion jeans and tops. If you don't know the stitches, get someone to show you.

A well-padded ironing board will help you do a professional job of pressing. No need to send out.

To hold lingerie straps in place, cut a small piece of tape, either bias or straight (about 2 in. long), and fold it in half lengthwise. Fold in the ends, and stitch across each end. Sew the bottom half of a snap to each end, and sew the two other halves to the shoulder seam inside the dress. To enclose the lingerie straps with the strap holder, snap it in place and straps will stay put.

Whenever possible, insert zippers in skirts and necklines before closing side seams. It is much easier to do then because you can spread the garment flat.

Perhaps you can save buying a new zipper by reusing an old one. If it is too long, cut it off to the proper length for the neck or skirt opening. Sew it in place. When you finish the neck or skirt opening, sew across the top of the zipper, thus making a place for the zipper tab to stop. (Warning: Be sure not to close your zipper all the way before you have finished sewing across the top of it, or you will pull off the tab and ruin the zipper.)

When making draperies, baste in a temporary hem and let them hang for at least two weeks before putting in the permanent hem. Trim the bottoms where they have sagged and hem. This will prevent an uneven hemline.

To cover cording for a long waistline tie for a dress or top do this: For ¼ in. cording, cut the material 2 in. wide and as long as you want your tie to be. Use a length of cording twice as long as you want your finished tie to be. Find the midway point of the cording, and fold the material around it with the wrong side out. With a ⅝ in. wide seam, stitch across the end of the material at this midway point, securing it to the cording. Stitch all the way down the side, seaming the material together and enclosing the cording (Fig. 22-2). Now pull on the end of the cording you have just covered while you gradually roll the material back over the other half of the cording. (When you are finished turning the material right side out, you will have covered the opposite half of the cording.)

Save all sewing scraps for baby and doll quilts. They make great gifts for new mothers and little girls.

To finish raw edges when sewing on leather such as at the neck, bottom, and armholes, cut ½ in. wide strips of leather in the length needed and stitch them to the garment with the wrong sides together on the edge to be finished. Now make a second stitching along the opposite edge of your ½ in. wide leather facing. Your finished edges will still be raw, but you will have a professional-looking doublestitched finish for your hem, armholes, and neck.

Do you bind double-fold bias tape to garments with one stitching? You should. Look carefully and you will see that one side of the bias tape is just a shade narrower than the opposite side. Fold the tape over the edge to be bound with the

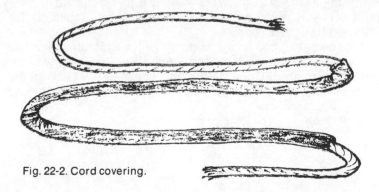

Fig. 22-2. Cord covering.

narrowest edge on the top side of your material. Bow, being careful to enclose the raw edge in the double fold of the binding; topstitch. One stitching will catch in both sides of the tape.

If you are making your own lingerie, use sharp shears. Some women prefer barber shears.

Silk pins are better for pinning lingerie fabrics and other synthetic knits.

Do you know about lingerie patterns that come multiple-sized so that, for example, just one pattern will make panties in sizes 4 through 9?

Use polyester thread for synthetic knits.

Use ballpoint needles in your machine for knits.

If you are sewing on tubular rib knits do not lay your pattern on the fold because sometimes that fold will not iron out. Instead, refold the material so that the original fold is in the middle; then cut (anything required to be cut on the fold) on the fold you made.

When sewing on single-knit tubular jerseys with a straight stitch machine, stretch the material a little as you sew to give the illusion of the elasticity of a zigzag stitch. (The material will spring back into shape if you do not stretch too hard.)

Do you have a coat or jacket lining that has worn out along the hemline? Match the lining as well as you can, and buy the amount of material needed to replace the lining from under the armholes to the hemline. Cut off the old lining about 3 in. below the armholes but do not cut right up to the front facings. Leave about 1½ in. of old lining still attached to the coat facings so that you will have something to sew your new lining to. Use the old fronts and backs of lining for patterns to cut new pieces. Press and allow for seams. Allow an extra 1 in. on fronts where you will attach them to the old strip of lining you have left there. Allow for seaming at the top of the new lining and for hemming at the bottom. When you have joined the old and the new across the coat beneath the armholes, topstitch for greater strength if you like.

If you have gone on a sewing binge for a month or so, then it is time to clean your sewing machine of accumulated lint. Wipe and brush it. Get out your instruction booklet and oil the machine according to directions. You will be repaid in a longer life for your machine.

Index